# the whole smiths
## GOOD FOOD COOKBOOK

For information about permission to reproduce selections from this book, write
to trade.permissions@hmhco.com or to Permissions, Houghton Mifflin Harcourt
Publishing Company, 3 Park Avenue, 19th Floor, New York, New York 10016.

hmhco.com

Library of Congress Cataloging-in-Publication Data is available.

ISBN 978-1-328-91509-2 (hbk)

ISBN 978-1-328-91517-7 (ebk)


Book design by Empire Design Studio

Printed in the United States of America

DOC 10 9 8 7 6 5 4 3 2

4500711010

To Camryn and Teagan:
May all your wildest dreams
come true. You are my everything.

# Contents

# ACKNOWLEDGMENTS

To Melissa Hartwig, thank you not only for creating and sharing your amazing program and food philosophy with the world, but for trusting and believing in me to be a part of it. My deepest gratitude will always be with you.

To my editor Justin Schwartz, thank you for your guidance and hard work on this project. I'm so grateful for your expertise. It's pushed me to be better than I was. Thank you for helping create the book I've been dreaming of for so long.

To Lisa Grubka and Christy Fletcher at Fletcher and Company, thank you both for all your hard work in putting this project together. Lisa, your guidance and insight on this book have been so valuable, thank you. You guys are rock stars, and I'm so flattered and happy to be part of your collective of authors.

To Brad, my favorite foodie: Your steadfast belief and excitement in what I'm doing means more than you'll ever know. Thank you for being the partner I always dreamed of and loving every crazy part of me. See you at the French Laundry!

To Mom and Dad, thank you for raising me with the value of healthy eating and always having a home-cooked meal set on the table for us growing up. And thank you, too, for all the time you've spent taking care of the girls to give me space to work on this project. I couldn't have done it without you.

To Beverly Floresca and Annie Bland, you guys have been with me from the start, and your love and unwavering support has meant the world to me. Thank you for being part of my world and for listening to my incessant yammering about all things food, blog, and book.

To my foodie twin, Teresa Langshaw, thank you for being my unofficial recipe tester. May we order the same meal at restaurants for many, many years to come.

To Kristen Boehmer, thank you for always being my sounding board, cheerleader, and confidante. I'm so thankful the universe brought us together and that we can share our journeys with each other.

To all my blogger friends, thank you for being my support system and the best "coworkers" a girl could ask for. Thank you to Anthropologie and my friends at American Heirloom for contributing such beautiful kitchenware to showcase my creations.

And last but not least, thank you to each and every person who has followed my recipes and shenanigans on social media and on my blog. Your comments and questions have fueled my passion, and I am forever thankful for your role in my journey.

# FOREWORD

I hate flipping through the pages of a gorgeous new cookbook, only to say, "This looks delicious, but there's no way I'd ever actually MAKE this food." Exotic ingredients, meticulous 27-step instructions, long cooking times . . . that's just not my life. I run my own business, am a single mom, really like exercise and sleep, and occasionally have to do laundry. I love to cook, but the meals I make need to fit into my daily schedule, check all my nutrition boxes, and pass the five-year-old's taste test.

These are all things Michelle Smith *totally* gets.

When I first discovered @thewholesmiths on Instagram, my first thought was, "This woman is REAL." She wasn't afraid to talk about the messy, imperfect parts of running a household and feeding her family—hallelujah. Then, I started looking at her food. Oh, the FOOD. Buffalo Chicken Sweet Potato Bites, a Whole Roasted Chicken that actually looked attainable, Awesome Sauce that turns any green vegetable into Something My Child Will Eat, and . . . wait, are those . . . ROSÉ Gummies? (Hey, it's not the Whole365, and in my food freedom, a little rosé is A-OK.)

Michelle's food ticks all my boxes: healthy, realistic, delicious, and fun. There are lots of Whole30-compliant recipes, but plenty of variety for *your* food freedom. And it's stuff I can actually pull off on a richly scheduled day; whole-food, nutritious meals that also taste fantastic—even if we ARE eating off paper plates.

I'm beyond excited to introduce you to Michelle's style, food, and humor in the first ever Whole30 Endorsed cookbook. Just keep reading and you'll see exactly what I mean.

Best in health,

**Melissa Hartwig**
**Whole30 Headmistress**

# INTRODUCTION

Growing up in the eighties and nineties, my family always ate "healthy," or what I like to call "eighties/nineties healthy." Butter was banished from our refrigerator, white bread was unheard of, and I never once tasted whole milk. We always had a nice tub of margarine in the fridge, lots of whole wheat bread for turkey and American cheese sandwiches, and a boatload of nonfat milk. It was oatmeal for breakfast, sandwiches for lunch, and pasta and frozen vegetables for dinner. We even spent some time as vegetarians.

Don't get me wrong—there are worse ways to eat, and we definitely weren't the unhealthiest family on the block. But what we know about nutrition and what helps our bodies function properly today is vastly different from what we knew back then.

Today, I focus on making meals for my family that are rich in fresh produce, high-quality proteins, and healthy fats. With that said, we're still busy people with jobs, school, activities, and, well, lives outside the kitchen. My children love sweets and snacks, I love being able to make a meal quickly, and my husband just likes to eat.

This cookbook was designed with on-the-go people like us in mind. The recipes I've created use easy-to-source ingredients and simple cooking techniques to make healthy food with lots of flavor. Long gone are the days when healthy eating meant a boiled skinless chicken breast and a bowl of steamed broccoli. These recipes are amazingly delicious and made to keep your attention in the long run.

Welcome to your new healthy.

xoxo,
michelle

# MY FOOD FREEDOM

As is the case with so many new parents, when my children were born, the world suddenly became a dangerous place. We're inundated with frightening warnings on everything from crib bumpers to pacifiers, television, and more. Everything had a danger warning attached to it. What on earth was I thinking, bringing children into this hostile environment?

Out of that new-found fear bloomed a concern about the types of food my family and I were eating. With so many "diets" out there, figuring out what should end up on our kitchen table raised a lot of questions: Should we become vegan? Was this gluten-free thing a fad? What the heck did "Paleo" even mean?

After much research, I decided that a diet full of minimally processed foods made the most sense to me and chose to give Paleo a go . . . once I finally figured out what it was, of course.

When I first made the commitment to clean up my diet and "eat Paleo," I figured I'd be swearing off all sorts of foods for the rest of my life. Pizza, beer, and ice cream would be a thing of the past, I thought. Thing is, I lasted three days before I dove headfirst into a giant plate of French fries and ranch dressing, which left me feeling utterly discouraged with a sense of failure. I wasn't sure where all this left me. As a self-proclaimed foodie, I loved a lot of different types of food; I couldn't be this discriminatory with it, and there was no way I would be able to maintain such a black-and-white diet for The. Rest. Of. My. Life. If I was going to be overcome with guilt every time I ate gluten, cheese, or sugar, this wasn't going to work for me.

Despite my setback, I kept going. And I screwed up a lot. But still, I kept going. Changes came slowly but naturally. I wasn't buying as much yogurt and cheese on my grocery runs, and I started replacing the sliced bread for my sandwiches with slabs of peppers and cucumbers. I slowed down on soda before eliminating it altogether. As I pushed through the screw-ups, I started making more and more healthy changes.

Several months into my journey toward healthier eating, I came across the Whole30 on Instagram and decided to try it out. At that point, I'd cleaned up enough of my diet to understand what I would need to do, so it wouldn't be such a stretch, would it?

Well, I didn't complete my first round. Womp womp. It's safe to say it was a bit tougher than I thought.

I tried again, with better planning, and made it through. And, like so many others who've completed the program, I felt amazing. For someone who had spent their entire life saying they had bad skin, mine looked fantastic.

Unbeknownst to me, I actually had great skin. I had energy and felt like the person I always thought I should be. I didn't go into a food coma after a big meal but instead actually felt replenished. My mood improved, and I finally felt . . . healthy.

Aside from the external and internal benefits of the program, I also identified some of my food sensitivities. At this point, I've cut out gluten completely and limit my dairy and sugar intake. A small amount of legumes and gluten-free grains don't bother me all that much, but my stomach throws a hissy fit when I consume those foods in larger quantities.

With Whole30, I've been able to identify the foods that make my body unhappy and create a custom diet around the principles laid out in the program.

I wrote this cookbook to fit your personal Food Freedom and whatever that entails. Even though every recipe is gluten-free (I needed to taste the darn things, after all!), most are customizable. Much of the book is either Whole30-compliant or can be easily modified to be compliant. Grains appear sparingly, and most of the recipes don't require dairy. I give you options for dairy-free alternatives such as almond-based milks, yogurts, and cheeses, but you can always stick with traditional dairy products if you're fine with dairy or avoiding nuts. The choice is yours, depending on your Food Freedom.

A number of these recipes use ingredients that are Whole30-compliant but would fall under the SWYPO (Sex with Your Pants On*) category if consumed on the program. You might find that they're perfectly acceptable in your Food Freedom, or you might find that those SWYPO recipes trigger old habits and you need to skip them. Again, the choice is yours.

Today, my Food Freedom consists of a lot of Whole30-compliant meals, homemade pizza nights with the family, a couple of cocktails when I'm out with friends, and froyo with my little girls after their soccer game. I still enjoy treats, but that's just what they are: treats. They don't make up the majority of my diet anymore, so I eat them guilt-free (for the most part), knowing that most of my diet is composed of fresh vegetables, high-quality proteins, and healthy fats.

*Sex with Your Pants On: The Paleo-ification of comfort foods like pizza, pancakes, and cookies using Whole30-compliant ingredients. For a comprehensive explanation of and answers to all your questions about SWYPO, visit Whole30.com.

My Food Freedom

# KIDS AND FOOD

One of the most common questions I get is, "Do your kids eat like you do?" The short answer is yes. When we're at home, we have the same meals and the same snacks, and share the same pantry.

I'm not a fan of making separate meals for my kids, and I know when they genuinely dislike something versus when they're just in the mood to complain. I don't worry about what they eat when they're at birthday parties or celebrating special occasions at school, because I know that most of what they're eating comes from home and is healthy.

I'm acutely aware of raising two young girls in today's image-driven society and am cautious about the dangers of demonizing any sort of food. I want to raise girls who know what it's like to eat healthy food that fuels your body but also know that it's okay to include some sweets and treats occasionally.

How you decide to present food choices to your children is your call, but I leave you with this thought: As parents, it's our job to teach our children values. Put it this way—if your child said they didn't want to finish their homework, would you let them turn it in incomplete day after day? Probably not, because their schoolwork is important. And so is their health.

The same way that you make sure your child completes their homework, you teach them the importance of taking care of and respecting their bodies. Trust me—I know firsthand that it's not fun to listen to your toddler whine that they'd rather have cereal instead of eggs early in the morning, but I see it as my job as a parent to give my kids tools to make healthy choices for the years to come.

# PANTRY STAPLES

There are certain ingredients I always keep on hand as staples for quick and tasty meals. These essentials will be a huge help as you cook your way through this book.

**ALMOND MILK—**In lieu of dairy-based milks, my family frequently uses almond milk. Note, however, that all almond milks are not created equal. Many almond milks are processed with artificial thickeners and preservatives. You can either make your own or stick to brands that use minimal and clean ingredients. New Barn Organic Almondmilk, for example, is a great Whole30-compliant choice.

**GROUND CHIPOTLE—**You can find ground chipotle chiles in the Latino foods section of your grocery store. If you can't find ground chipotle, you can use the adobo sauce from canned chipotle peppers in its place. As usual, check your labels—not all canned chipotles are Whole30-compliant.

**COCONUT AMINOS—**I don't tend to cook with soy these days, so traditional soy sauce is out and coconut aminos are in. Derived from coconuts, aminos lend a salty, smoky flavor to your dishes.

**COCONUT MILK—**Read your labels! With the rise of everything coconut these days, there's a large variety of coconut milks on the market. Make sure that what you're buying is indeed pure coconut milk (a little added water is fine, but anything else is a no-go). I prefer canned full-fat coconut milk.

**GHEE—**Also known as clarified butter. Simply put, the butter gets melted down and simmered until the milk solids rise and get skimmed from the top. What's left is a flavorful cooking oil with a high smoke point. You can make this at home or buy it at the grocery store. I use it interchangeably with regular butter.

**LEMON PEPPER—**I love traditional black pepper, but lemon pepper gives any dish a boost of zest and an extra layer of flavor. Check your labels; some lemon pepper contains sugar. Trader Joe's carries a great Whole30-compliant version.

**SALT—**I prefer to use kosher or sea salt for my everyday cooking, and the recipes in this book use just that. If you choose to use a different type of salt, be aware that some salts are more potent than others, so adjust your salt accordingly. For an extra pop of flavor, I love to use flaky finishing salt (I like Maldon), which you can find at most grocery stores or online.

# KITCHEN TOOLS

I'm not going to reinvent the wheel and tell you the importance of stocking your kitchen with things like measuring cups and spoons. You've already got that on lock. But the tools listed here are some gadgets that you may not already own but that will make your cooking adventures quicker and easier.

**FOOD SCALE—**I can't believe I've become one of those food nerds with a kitchen scale, but it's a must-have for me now. I can't stress enough how important it is to weigh out meat and vegetables to ensure your recipes turn out the best they can.

**GARLIC TWIST—**I love the flavor of freshly minced garlic, but I hate how stinky it leaves my fingers. This gadget makes stinky garlic fingers a thing of the past while also mincing garlic with just a few quick twists.

**GREENS AND HERB STRIPPER—**I recently discovered this handy tool and already can't imagine my kitchen life without it. Instead of trimming greens and herbs by hand, I swipe them through this tool to strip their leaves in one fell swoop. I particularly love it for kale.

**HAND/IMMERSION BLENDER—**I used my hand blender solely for mixing up soups when I first got it, but now use it almost exclusively to make my 1-Minute Mayonnaise (page 195). It's also fantastic for dressings and beverages. This tool is a need-to-have for the 1-Minute Mayonnaise, and it's well worth it in the $20 to $30 price range.

**INSTANT POT—**Out of all the kitchen gadgets listed here, the game-changer award goes to the Instant Pot. It's an easy-to-use pressure cooker that enables me to "slow cook" recipes in a fraction of the time that an actual slow cooker would take. For someone with minimal plan-ahead skills, I'm all in. While some of the recipes in this book are designed for you to make with an Instant Pot, I always provide alternative instructions for traditional slow cookers—just be prepared to wait!

**KITCHEN SHEARS—**You do know that those scissors that came with your knife set aren't just for cutting open cereal boxes, right? I use my kitchen shears ALL. THE. TIME. They make cutting salmon fillets, bacon, and excess skin and fat from meat so much easier. I even use them in lieu of knives when chopping veggies and herbs like kale and chives. So stop using them to bust open bags of snacks, and start using them as a proper kitchen tool!

**MICROPLANE/RASP GRATER—**This tool will give you perfect grated lemon zest, freshly ground nutmeg, and finely grated ginger and turmeric. I use it all the time, and you will, too.

**DIGITAL MEAT THERMOMETER—**It's time to take the guessing out of your meat game. Since every piece of meat is cut differently and not every oven is calibrated the same, cook times are going to vary. Rather than cooking to time, cook to temp. A handy kitchen thermometer will tell you everything you need to know to ensure perfectly cooked proteins.

the whole smiths

# Breakfast + Brunch

# Sweet Potato Hash

**Serves 4**

½ pound thick-cut bacon, chopped

½ cup chopped yellow onion (about ½ medium)

1 red bell pepper, diced

2 medium sweet potatoes, peeled and grated (about 5 cups)

Salt and freshly ground black pepper

¼ teaspoon avocado oil or extra-virgin olive oil

4 large eggs

Hot sauce (optional)

There was a point in time when I ate this for breakfast four out of seven days a week. No joke—it's that good. But like everything else, I realized I needed some hash moderation, and these days, my consumption is down to once a week.

You can make a batch of this sweet potato hash ahead of time to use for breakfasts throughout the week; simply top it with a fried egg (or two) after you reheat it, and you're ready to go.

In a large skillet over medium heat, cook the bacon until lightly crisped, 5 to 7 minutes. Use a slotted spoon to transfer the bacon to a paper towel–lined plate or cutting board. Drain all but 1 tablespoon of the bacon grease from the pan into a heatproof glass container.

Add the onion to the skillet with the bacon grease and cook over medium heat, stirring, for 4 minutes. Add the bell pepper and cook, stirring, until the pepper and onion are tender, 3 to 4 minutes. Add 1 teaspoon of the reserved bacon grease to the pan, then add the grated sweet potatoes. Cook, stirring, until the sweet potatoes are tender and cooked through, 10 minutes. Return the bacon to the pan and stir to combine. Season with salt and black pepper and divide the hash among four plates.

In a medium nonstick skillet over medium heat, heat the avocado oil. Crack each egg gently into the pan and cook until the white is opaque and the yolk is set, 1 to 2 minutes.

Place an egg on top of each serving of hash. Serve with hot sauce, if you like.

**Tip** *Grate additional sweet potatoes and store them in a plastic zip-top bag in the refrigerator for up to 4 days. It makes prep that much easier if you're planning to make this breakfast multiple times a week.*

Paleo

Whole30

Gluten-Free

Dairy-Free

Nut-Free

# Apple French Toast

Serves 2 to 4

2 large eggs

½ cup almond flour

2 tablespoons unsweetened
almond milk

1 tablespoon pure maple syrup,
plus more for serving

Pinch of salt

1 tablespoon coconut oil

2 Granny Smith apples, peeled, cored,
and sliced into ¼-inch-thick discs

2 bananas, sliced

½ cup fresh sliced strawberries,
blueberries, and/or
raspberries, for serving

Even though I consider myself a "savory" breakfast person, I've always enjoyed a good lightly sweetened French toast. But trying to find one that's gluten-free? That gets a little tricky. I mean, how can you have French toast without the *toast*? With apples! That's how. Rather than dipping bread into egg, you can use the same technique with apple slices and a light egg batter. It's a great way to get all the flavors of French toast sans gluten.

In a large bowl, combine the eggs, almond flour, almond milk, maple syrup, and salt and whisk until thoroughly combined.

In a large nonstick skillet over medium-high heat, melt the coconut oil. Dip each apple disc into the batter to coat completely and let a bit of the excess drip off. Carefully lay the coated apple slices in the pan in a single layer and cook until they are lightly golden brown, 2 to 3 minutes. Using a metal spatula, very carefully flip the slices over and cook for 2 to 3 minutes more.

To assemble each "toast," set an apple disc on a plate and top with 4 banana slices in a single layer. Top that stack with another apple disc, 4 more banana slices, and a final apple disc. Repeat with the remaining apple and banana.

Serve with the berries and additional maple syrup.

**Tip** *I like to use a metal spatula to flip the apples to ensure the delicate batter stays on the apple. Just be careful not to scratch the nonstick cooking surface of your pan.*

Paleo
Gluten-Free
Vegetarian
Dairy-Free

# Sheet Pan Hash Browns

Serves 4

1½ pounds frozen shredded hash
browns, thawed and excess
liquid squeezed out

¾ cup freshly grated Pecorino
Romano cheese

1 cup chopped yellow onion
(about 1 medium)

5 tablespoons salted butter
or ghee, melted

1¼ teaspoons salt

¾ teaspoon garlic powder

¾ teaspoon freshly ground
black pepper

6 large eggs

2 medium tomatoes, sliced,
for serving

2 scallions, thinly sliced, for serving

4 fresh basil leaves, chopped,
for serving

Red pepper flakes, for serving
(optional)

Am I the only one who can't get a consistent, crispy 'do on my hash browns if I make them in a skillet? Turns out, there's a better way: in the oven.

Preheat the oven to 425°F. Line a large baking sheet with parchment paper.

In a large bowl, combine the hash browns, cheese, onion, melted butter, salt, garlic powder, and black pepper and stir until well incorporated.

Spread the hash brown mixture into a thin, even layer on the prepared baking sheet and bake for 20 minutes. Move the pan to sit directly under the broiler and switch the oven to broil for 1 to 2 minutes, until the tops of the hash browns are golden and crispy.

Return the oven to 425°F.

Remove the pan from the oven and carefully create six 2-inch-wide wells in the hash browns, spacing them evenly apart. Gently crack an egg into each well and return the pan to the oven. Bake for 10 to 12 minutes, until the egg whites are set and the yolks are soft.

To serve, top the hash browns with the scallions, tomato slices, basil, and a sprinkling of red pepper flakes, if desired.

Gluten-Free
Vegetarian
Nut-Free

# Chipotle Breakfast Tostada

Serves 4 to 6

**For the sweet potatoes:**

2 small sweet potatoes, peeled and cut into bite-size pieces

2 teaspoons extra-virgin olive oil

¼ teaspoon smoked paprika

¼ teaspoon salt

**For the beans:**

2 teaspoons extra-virgin olive oil

2 garlic cloves, minced

1 (15-ounce) can black beans, drained and rinsed

½ teaspoon smoked paprika

½ teaspoon salt

**To assemble:**

1 tablespoon plus 2 teaspoons extra-virgin olive or avocado oil

½ pound fresh (Mexican) chorizo

6 corn tortillas

6 large eggs

¼ cup chopped fresh cilantro

3 radishes, thinly sliced

1 jalapeño, thinly sliced

2 tablespoons chopped red onion

½ recipe Chipotle Crema (page 208)

In our house, we love breakfast, and we love Mexican food. So whenever we have a chance to combine both, we do. And it's always a good day when that happens.

**For the sweet potatoes:** Preheat the oven to 425°F. Line two large baking sheets with parchment paper.

In a large bowl, combine the sweet potatoes, olive oil, paprika, and salt and toss to coat. Divide the sweet potatoes between the prepared baking sheets and arrange them in a single layer. Bake for 25 minutes.

**For the beans:** In a medium saucepan over medium heat, heat the olive oil. Add the garlic and cook, stirring, until fragrant, about 1 minute. Add the black beans, paprika, and salt and reduce the heat to low. Simmer until the beans are heated through, about 5 minutes, and set aside.

**To assemble:** In large skillet over medium heat, heat 1 teaspoon of the olive oil. Add the chorizo and cook, gently breaking it up with a spatula, until it is cooked through, 5 to 7 minutes.

In a small skillet over medium heat, heat 1 tablespoon of the olive oil. Cook the tortillas one at a time until lightly browned, 30 seconds to 1 minute on each side. Drain each tortilla on a paper towel–lined cutting board or plate and let cool.

In the same pan you used for the tortillas, heat the remaining 1 teaspoon olive oil over medium heat. Fry each egg for about 1 minute, until the white is set but the yolk is still runny.

To build the tostadas, layer each tortilla with the sweet potatoes, beans, chorizo, and a fried egg. Top with the cilantro, radish, jalapeño, and onion. Drizzle with Chipotle Crema and serve immediately.

 *To modify for Whole30, skip the corn tortillas and beans, toss it all into a bowl, and grab a fork instead!*

Whole30-Compliant if Modified

Gluten-Free

Dairy-Free

Nut-Free

# Almond Chia Pudding

2 cups unsweetened almond milk

1½ tablespoons honey

¼ teaspoon ground cinnamon

¼ teaspoon pure vanilla extract

¼ teaspoon pure almond extract

6 tablespoons chia seeds

¼ cup sliced almonds

I really do love some me some chia pudding. Whether it's a breakfast or an afternoon snack, it always hits the spot. It's also convenient when you're on the go. I often pour chia pudding into mason jars, baby food jars, or even squeeze pouches. Bring along a spoon, and you're all set!

In a large bowl, combine the almond milk, honey, cinnamon, vanilla, and almond extract. Whisk until the honey has dissolved, about 2 minutes. Add the chia seeds and whisk vigorously for 2 minutes more, or until the pudding mixture starts to thicken. Add the sliced almonds and stir to combine.

Pour the pudding equally into two individual jars, cover, and chill for 6 hours, or until set.

Paleo

Gluten-Free

Vegan

Vegetarian

Dairy-Free

# Strawberry Protein Chia Custard

## Serves 2

10 large fresh strawberries, hulled

1 cup unsweetened almond milk

2 large eggs

2 tablespoons honey

1 teaspoon pure vanilla extract

½ cup chia seeds

1 teaspoon unsweetened shredded coconut, for garnish

1 teaspoon ground golden flaxseed, for garnish

While I adore how easy it is to whip up chia puddings for a quick breakfast or snack, but sometimes I wish there was a bit more protein in them. So I took matters into my own hands and decided to turn my "pudding" into a protein-packed "custard" with the simple addition of some eggs. It's an easy update, and you're sure to love the creamy, rich results!

Put 8 of the strawberries in a blender and blend on high until pureed. Add the almond milk, eggs, honey, and vanilla and blend on high until the mixture is combined and smooth.

Carefully pour the strawberry mixture into a medium saucepan over medium-low heat. Cook, whisking continuously, until the eggs are cooked through evenly, about 4 minutes. The mixture will be slightly frothy.

Return the strawberry mixture to the blender. Add the chia seeds and pulse until just incorporated. Pour the custard base into two small bowls. Cover with plastic wrap and refrigerate for at least 6 hours or up to overnight, until set.

To serve, slice the remaining strawberries and sprinkle them over the top of the custard, along with the shredded coconut and ground flaxseeds.

Paleo
Gluten-Free
Dairy-Free
Vegetarian

# Chicken, Pesto + Sun-Dried Tomato Egg "Pizzas"

Serves 4 to 6

**For the pesto:**

¾ cup extra-virgin olive oil

1 cup packed fresh basil leaves

¼ cup pine nuts

¼ cup salted cashews

½ teaspoon salt

**To assemble:**

Extra-virgin olive oil

8 large eggs, beaten

1 cup shredded cooked chicken
(light and dark meat)

½ cup sun-dried tomatoes, chopped

Pine nuts, for garnish (optional)

Through my food blogging journey, I've met lots of other food lovers and bloggers. Kristen of Living, Loving, Paleo (livinglovingpaleo.com) has been particularly inspiring to me. Whether it's treating her Crohn's disease through food or being a ninja in and out of the kitchen (yes, she really does Ninja Warrior training!), Kristen is living proof that food is power and that we are all in control of our health.

Kristen is also the master of delicious, healthy breakfasts. So when I was thinking about Whole30 breakfast recipes for this book, I called her up to join me in the kitchen. The result is this amazing dish. The brilliant flavor combo was all her, and it's so good you'll be tempted to eat the entire batch.

The secret to these egg "pizzas" lies in the mini nonstick egg pans we used. They fit exactly one scrambled egg and make the perfect base for any sort of "pizza." You can find them at most kitchen supply stores or on Amazon.

**For the pesto:** In a blender or food processor, combine the olive oil, basil, pine nuts, cashews, and salt and blend on high or process for 30 seconds, or until the pesto is well combined but not perfectly smooth. Set aside.

**To assemble:** In a nonstick 4½-inch egg skillet over medium-low heat, heat ¼ teaspoon olive oil. Pour in enough of the beaten egg to coat the bottom of the pan and cook until the edges start to round, 1 to 2 minutes. Flip the egg and cook until the edges are slightly golden and the egg is cooked through, 20 to 30 seconds. Transfer to a plate and repeat with the remaining egg.

To serve, spread 2 tablespoons of the pesto onto each cooked egg round and top with about 2 tablespoons of the shredded chicken and 1 to 2 teaspoons of the sun-dried tomatoes. Garnish with pine nuts, if desired.

Paleo
Whole30
Gluten-Free
Dairy-Free

GREAT FOR LEFTOVERS!
★ ★ ★

# Spicy Harissa Shakshuka

**Serves 4 to 6**

1 tablespoon extra-virgin olive oil

1 medium yellow onion, chopped (about 1 cup)

1 teaspoon salt

4 garlic cloves, minced

1 (14.5-ounce) can diced tomatoes

½ cup harissa (I like Mina)

1 (6-ounce) can tomato paste

4 or 5 saffron threads

4 cups loosely packed baby spinach

4 large eggs

1 tablespoon chopped fresh parsley, for serving

*Shakshuka* is a traditional dish of eggs poached in a flavorful tomato sauce commonly found in Northern African and Middle Eastern cuisines. Not only is it quite delicious, but it's also amazingly easy to make. Never one to leave well enough alone, I just had to tinker with the original by adding some harissa and saffron—the perfect additional dimension of flavor. This dish is a bit spicy, so make sure to add less of the harissa or omit it altogether if you have little ones.

In a large skillet over medium heat, heat the olive oil. Add the onion and salt and cook, stirring frequently, until the onion is tender, 8 to 10 minutes. Add the garlic and cook, stirring, for 1 minute more. Stir in the diced tomatoes, harissa, tomato paste, saffron, and ½ cup water. Bring the sauce to a simmer and cook for 3 to 4 minutes, then, one at a time, crack each egg into the sauce, spacing them evenly apart. Cover the pan and cook the shakshuka until the egg whites are set and the yolks are cooked to your liking, 8 to 10 minutes.

Serve with the parsley sprinkled on top.

Paleo

Whole30

Gluten-Free

Vegetarian

Dairy-Free

Nut-Free

# No'tmeal

Serves 1 to 2

1 large banana

½ cup unsweetened almond milk

¼ cup almond meal (see Note)

¼ cup raw cashew pieces

¼ cup unsweetened shredded coconut

1 tablespoon ground golden flaxseed

½ teaspoon ground cinnamon

2 tablespoons toppings of your choice, such as blueberries, walnut pieces, or dried fruit (without added sugar)

Some mornings, the only thing that can pry me out of my warm, cozy sheets is the promise of an equally warm and cozy breakfast. Prior to switching over to a cleaner diet, that often meant a bowl of piping-hot oatmeal with all the fixings. It was the ultimate breakfast comfort food. When you're avoiding grains, though, joining the warm and cozy oatmeal club might not be an option. Until now! This bowl of No'tmeal brings all the warm fuzzies, sans the grains. You can serve it as is, zap it in the microwave for 20 seconds, and top it with your favorite oatmeal accessories.

In a blender, combine the banana, almond milk, almond meal, cashew pieces, coconut, flaxseed, and cinnamon and blend on high for 10 to 15 seconds. The No'tmeal should have a slightly lumpy texture.

To serve, pour into a bowl (or divide between two bowls) and sprinkle with the toppings of your choice.

Note *If almond meal is unavailable, you can use use almond flour in its place. The texture will be slightly different, but still delicious.*

Paleo

Gluten-Free

Vegan

Vegetarian

Dairy-Free

# Smoked Salmon Sweet Potato Toast

## Serves 4

½ cup plain cream cheese (dairy-free or regular), at room temperature

1½ teaspoons chopped fresh dill, plus more for serving

1 teaspoon chopped fresh chives, plus more for serving

1 teaspoon capers, drained and rinsed, plus more for serving

⅛ teaspoon fresh lemon juice

1 large sweet potato, cut lengthwise into ¼-inch-thick slices

4 ounces smoked salmon

Not a lot of people can say they know someone who invented something, but I can! My friend Kelsey over at Little Bits of Real Food (littlebitsof.com) was the mastermind behind the sweet potato toast that took the Internet by storm in 2016. The OG sweet potato toast, if you will. This recipe is an ode to Kelsey's creativity and kitchen prowess. This version takes the traditional flavors of smoked salmon, cream cheese, capers, chives, and fresh dill and packs it onto one amazing piece of "toast."

In a small bowl, combine the cream cheese, dill, chives, capers, and lemon juice. Mix well and set aside.

Toast the sweet potato slices on high in a toaster for two or three cycles, until the slices soften and start to brown around the edges.

Spread 2 tablespoons of the cream cheese mixture onto each sweet potato slice and top with 1 ounce of the smoked salmon.

Serve with additional chives, dill, and capers sprinkled on top.

**Tip** *Try to find a sweet potato with a wide circumference. The wider the potato, the easier it will be to slice lengthwise, and the bigger the surface area will be for your toppings.*

Paleo
Gluten-Free
Dairy-Free

# Banana Eggs

Serves 4

3 medium bananas

7 large eggs

½ teaspoon ground cinnamon

Pinch of salt

1 tablespoon coconut oil

1 cup fresh blueberries, for serving

½ cup unsweetened shredded coconut, for serving

2 tablespoons ground golden flaxseed, for serving

Banana Eggs?! Say whaaat? Think of this as the beautiful love child of a failed banana pancake and oatmeal. This has been an amazing way to get my kiddos (and me) to eat eggs in the morning when we are Sick. Of. Eggs. We top them with all sorts of berries, nuts, and seeds, so feel free to tinker around to find a combination that you love.

In a medium bowl, mash the bananas with a fork or potato masher until they have the consistency of a thick batter. Set aside.

In separate medium bowl, beat together the eggs, cinnamon, and salt. Set aside.

In a large nonstick skillet over medium heat, melt the coconut oil. Add the mashed bananas and cook, gently stirring, until heated through, 2 to 3 minutes. Add the egg mixture to the pan and use a spatula to scramble it with the banana mash. Cook until the eggs are cooked and not runny, about 5 minutes.

To serve, divide the banana eggs among four plates and top with the blueberries, coconut, and flaxseed.

Paleo
Vegetarian
Gluten-Free
Dairy-Free
Nut-Free

# Brussels Sprout Hash

### Serves 4

1 tablespoon plus 1 teaspoon extra-virgin olive or avocado oil, salted butter, or ghee, plus more as needed

¾ cup chopped red onion (about ¾ medium)

1 red bell pepper, diced

6 cups shredded Brussels sprouts

1 teaspoon salt

½ teaspoon lemon pepper

4 large eggs

Hot sauce (optional)

This is one of our family's favorite breakfasts, and it's a breeze to whip up on busy mornings. It loads you up on healthy fats, green veggies, and some protein, all before you even walk out the door. This recipe was inspired by Natalie's Brussels Sprout Hash and Buckwheat Crepe recipe over at *Perry's Plate* (perrysplate.com). Years ago, it was the first recipe I made from any blog . . . ever! Fast-forward to today, and I am happy to call Natalie a friend and one of my favorite bloggers.

I like to make a large batch of the Brussels sprouts to use for breakfasts throughout the week. Simply reheat the Brussels hash and top it with a fried egg to save some time.

In a large skillet over medium-high heat, heat 1 tablespoon of the olive oil. Add the onion and bell pepper and cook, stirring, until tender, 5 to 7 minutes. Transfer the vegetables to a medium bowl and set aside.

Add the Brussels sprouts, salt, and lemon pepper to the skillet. Cook until the Brussels sprouts are tender and lightly browned around the edges, 5 to 7 minutes. Return the onions and bell pepper to the pan and stir to combine. Remove from the heat.

In a separate skillet over medium heat, heat the remaining 1 teaspoon oil. Add the eggs and fry for 1 minute on each side.

To serve, plate the Brussels sprouts, top with the fried eggs, and serve with hot sauce, if desired. Lay the fried eggs over the Brussels sprout hash and serve with hot sauce, if desired.

Tip | *To get quick shaved Brussels sprouts, buy them preshredded or pulse in a food processor.*

Paleo

Whole30

Gluten-Free

Vegetarian

Dairy-Free

Nut-Free

# Reuben Eggs Benedict

Serves 4

4 cups frozen shredded hash browns, thawed and excess liquid squeezed out (see Tip)

10 tablespoons salted butter, melted

½ cup chopped yellow onion (about ½ medium)

¾ teaspoon salt

⅛ teaspoon freshly ground black pepper

¼ cup 1-Minute Mayonnaise (page 195)

2 teaspoons sweet pickle relish (see Tip)

1 teaspoon tomato paste

3 large egg yolks

1 tablespoon fresh lemon juice

Dash of hot sauce

½ pound sliced pastrami

1 medium tomato, sliced

1 cup baby spinach

1 cup sauerkraut

4 large eggs, poached (see Tip)

⅛ teaspoon smoked paprika

Everybody has a favorite breakfast go-to. Maybe you're a waffle gal, or maybe you're a huevos rancheros kinda guy. Me? I'm an eggs Benedict girl, which is why I was so heartbroken when avoiding gluten forced me to stop ordering it at restaurants. It was sad to stare at a menu and long for all the

Gluten-Free
Dairy-Free
Nut-Free

eggs Benedict options I couldn't have. Then it dawned on me: There was a way! Instead of loading all that Benedict goodness up on a biscuit, why not stack it on a heap of hash browns instead? From then on, my eggs Bene days were back.

Preheat the oven to 425°F. Line a large baking sheet with parchment paper.

In a large bowl, combine the hash browns, 2 tablespoons of the melted butter, the onion, ½ teaspoon of the salt, and the pepper. Spread the hash brown mixture into an even layer on the prepared baking sheet and bake for 20 minutes. Move the sheet directly under the broiler and switch the oven to broil. Broil for 1 to 2 minutes more, until the hash browns are lightly crisped and golden.

Form the "biscuits" by filling a 4-inch biscuit cutter with one-quarter of the baked hash browns. Repeat with the remaining hash browns to make 4 "biscuits" total. Set aside.

In a small bowl, combine the mayonnaise, relish, and tomato paste. Set aside.

In a blender, combine the egg yolks, lemon juice, and hot sauce. With the blender running on low speed, very slowly drizzle in the remaining 8 tablespoons (½ cup) melted butter. Blend until the hollandaise sauce has thickened slightly, about 2 minutes. Set aside.

To assemble, lay the slices in a medium skillet over medium-low heat. Add 2 tablespoons of water and cook until the pastrami is heated through, 1 to 2 minutes. Transfer the pastrami to a paper towel–lined plate.

Layer each hash brown "biscuit" with 1 tablespoon of the Reuben sauce, a tomato slice, ¼ cup of the baby spinach, ¼ cup of the sauerkraut, one-quarter of the pastrami, and a poached egg. Drizzle with the hollandaise, sprinkle with the smoked paprika, and serve.

> **Tip** *Beware of added artificial colors, high-fructose corn syrup, and chemicals when purchasing sweet pickle relish and frozen hash browns!*

> **Tip** *To poach the eggs, fill a stockpot halfway with water, add a dash of white or apple cider vinegar, and bring the water to a low simmer. Crack each egg individually into a small cup. Gently stir the simmering water to create a whirlpool motion in the pot and slowly pour in one egg at a time (don't crowd them). Cook the egg(s) for 3 to 4 minutes and remove with a slotted spoon. Place the poached eggs on paper towels to soak up any additional water.*

# Mixed Berry Frittata

### Serves 4 to 6

1 teaspoon coconut oil

1 Granny Smith apple, peeled, cored, and cut into ⅛-inch-thick slices

½ cup fresh raspberries, plus more for serving

½ cup fresh blueberries, plus more for serving

½ cup fresh blackberries, plus more for serving

10 large eggs

¼ cup honey

1 teaspoon pure vanilla extract

½ teaspoon ground cinnamon

In our family, this dish is lovingly known as the "fruit-tata," courtesy of my five-year-old, Teagan (I'm secretly jealous I didn't come up with that first). I know—fruit and eggs together sounds like a recipe for disaster, but you've got to hang with me on this one! The eggs are lightly sweetened with honey, which complements the tartness of the berries. It's the ultimate sweet(er) alternative to a savory breakfast.

Preheat the oven to 375°F. Lightly grease a 9-inch pie plate or ceramic baking dish with the coconut oil.

Layer the apple slices evenly over the bottom of the prepared pie plate. Scatter about half of the raspberries, blueberries, and blackberries over the apples.

In a large bowl, whisk together the eggs, honey, vanilla, and cinnamon until fully incorporated. Slowly pour the egg mixture over the fruit. Gently jiggle the plate to help the egg mixture settle into the dish. Scatter the remaining berries over the top.

Bake for 30 minutes, then let the frittata rest for 15 minutes. Serve with additional berries on top, if desired.

> **Tip** *Coat your measuring cup or spoon with coconut oil prior to measuring your honey to help it slide out more easily and avoid sticking. Perfect if you're impatient like me!*

Paleo
Gluten-Free
Vegetarian
Dairy-Free
Nut-Free

# Cloud Eggs Furikake

Serves 1 or 2

2 large eggs

⅛ teaspoon salt

¼ cup grated Pecorino Romano or Parmesan cheese

⅛ teaspoon furikake, for serving

Hot sauce, for serving

Don't be deceived by how pretty these eggs are—making them is quite simple, and anyone, I mean *anyone*, can do it. I like to use *furikake*, a Japanese seasoning traditionally used on rice, vegetables, and fish; it adds great umami to the eggs without overwhelming them. And because it seems impossible for me to enjoy eggs without hot sauce, I add a bit of that, too. Feel free to experiment with toppings like fresh chives, diced pancetta, black pepper, and red pepper flakes. This is even good on top of some avocado toast.

A note to all you single folks: I'll also go out on a limb and say that these would impress any overnight guest you may be having over. It just might convince them to stay over again, *if you know what I mean*. Just sayin'.

Preheat the oven to 450°F. Line a small baking sheet with parchment paper.

Separate the eggs, putting each egg yolk in its own small bowl and the egg whites in the bowl of a stand mixer fitted with the whisk attachment or a large bowl. Add the salt to the egg whites.

Whisk the egg whites on low speed until foamy. Raise the speed to medium-high and whisk until the egg whites hold stiff peaks, 4 to 5 minutes. Gently fold the cheese into the egg whites. Form two egg white "nests" on the prepared baking sheet, using half of the mixture for each. Use a (clean) finger to create a 1½-inch-wide well in the center of each nest, leaving the bottom intact, and bake for 3 minutes. Add an egg yolk to the center of each nest and bake for 3 minutes more.

Top with the furikake and hot sauce and serve.

**Note** To modify for Paleo or Whole30, omit the cheese and replace it with ¼ cup nutritional yeast.

Paleo If Modified

Whole30-Compliant If Modified

Gluten-Free

Vegetarian

Nut-Free

# Blackberry-Peach Oatmeal Bake

### Serves 4 to 6

1 teaspoon unsalted butter, ghee, or coconut oil, at room temperature, plus 4 tablespoons melted

1 yellow peach, peeled, pitted, and thinly sliced

2 cups gluten-free oats

1 teaspoon ground cinnamon

1 teaspoon baking powder

⅛ teaspoon salt

6 large eggs, beaten

1½ cups unsweetened almond milk

¼ cup pure maple syrup

1 cup fresh blackberries

My kids think this is called an oatmeal *cake*, and I never correct them. I figure the idea of cake for breakfast is part of the reason why they never, ever complain when we have this. I love it because it's easy to make the night before and reheat the next morning, and is super adaptable depending on your mood. You can try different fruit combinations, add a few more eggs for a boost of protein, flavor it with extra cinnamon, use less maple syrup, more maple syrup . . . you get the gist.

Preheat the oven to 375°F. Grease a 7 by 10-inch baking dish with 1 teaspoon room-temperature butter.

Line the bottom of the prepared baking dish with the peach slices and set aside.

In a large bowl, stir together the oats, cinnamon, baking powder, and salt.

In a medium bowl, whisk together the eggs, almond milk, maple syrup, and melted butter until well combined. Add the egg mixture to the oat mixture and stir to combine.

Pour the batter over the peaches to coat as evenly as possible. Some of the peaches may float to the surface, but that's okay! Evenly distribute the blackberries over the batter and bake for 35 minutes, until browned around the edges and the eggs are cooked through. Let rest for 10 minutes prior to serving. Slice to serve.

Gluten-Free

Vegetarian

# Easy Bake Egg Muffins

## Serves 3 or 4

1 teaspoon extra-virgin olive oil,
for greasing

6 slices prosciutto, halved

7 large eggs, beaten

½ red bell pepper, finely chopped

¼ cup chopped yellow onion
(about ¼ medium)

½ teaspoon salt

¼ teaspoon lemon pepper

This is the quintessential Whole30 recipe. It's easy to prepare, delicious, and makes for great leftovers. Not to mention they're portable, which makes them great for meals on the go.

Preheat the oven to 350°F. Lightly grease the inside of 12 silicone muffin molds with the olive oil.

Place a piece of prosciutto into each prepared muffin mold (it's okay if some hangs over the edges).

In a large bowl, stir together the eggs, bell pepper, onion, salt, and lemon pepper. Fill each muffin mold two-thirds of the way with the egg mixture.

Bake for 17 to 20 minutes, until cooked through. Let cool for 7 to 10 minutes. Unmold and serve. Store refrigerated in an airtight container up to 3 days.

Paleo

Whole30

Gluten-Free

Dairy-Free

Nut-Free

# Snacks + Appetizers

# Mini Hasselback Tots + Horseradish Dip

Serves 4 to 6

2 pounds tricolored new potatoes

2 tablespoons extra-virgin olive oil

1 teaspoon salt

½ cup 1-Minute Mayonnaise (page 195)

1 tablespoon prepared horseradish

⅛ teaspoon freshly ground black pepper

I could probably double this recipe and my family would *still* devour these in one sitting. In fact, this is my kids' favorite, which—seriously?! I make a zillion recipes, and they pick a roasted potato? In all fairness, these potatoes *are* pretty amazing. By slicing them up hasselback-style, you get some extra crispiness while still leaving the insides creamy, and the salt and pepper pair perfectly with the bite of the horseradish. Whether you make these to munch on while watching football or as a midweek dinner side, I can promise they'll be a hit at your house, too.

Preheat the oven to 425°F. Line two large baking sheets with parchment paper.

Using a sharp knife, make horizontal cuts ⅛ inch apart all the way across the top of each potato, making sure not to cut all the way through the potato. Put the sliced potatoes in a large bowl with the olive oil and ½ teaspoon of the salt. Toss to coat.

Place the potatoes on the prepared baking sheets and bake for 30 to 35 minutes, flipping halfway through, until they are crisp and lightly browned on the edges.

In a small bowl, combine the mayonnaise, horseradish, remaining ½ teaspoon salt, and the pepper and stir well.

Let the potatoes cool for 3 to 4 minutes prior to serving, as they will be quite hot. Serve with the horseradish dip alongside.

Whole30

Vegetarian

Dairy-Free

Nut-Free

# Grain-Free Popcorn Chicken

Serves 4

1½ pounds boneless, skin-on chicken breasts, cut into 1-inch pieces

2½ teaspoons salt, plus more for sprinkling

1½ cups almond flour

¼ cup plus 2 tablespoons tapioca flour

½ teaspoon smoked paprika

3 large eggs, beaten

1 cup coconut oil

Dairy-Free Magic Ranch (page 207), hot sauce, or Dijon mustard, for serving

Children of the last couple of decades have grown up on processed chicken cut into nuggets, tenders, strips, and, oddly enough, dinosaur shapes. They're ubiquitous—a staple on every children's menu across the country—and they deserve a healthy update. This recipe is grain-free, fried in coconut oil, and something you can feel good about giving your kids. The results are so dang tasty, though, that you might not even want to share. That's okay—I won't judge.

Season the chicken with 1½ teaspoons of the salt and set aside.

In a large bowl, combine the almond flour, tapioca flour, remaining 1 teaspoon salt, and the paprika. Pour the beaten eggs into a shallow bowl.

Dip the chicken in the egg, letting the excess drip off, then roll in the flour mixture to coat. Set aside.

In a large skillet or Dutch oven over medium heat, melt the coconut oil. Working in batches, fry the chicken until the crust is a light golden brown and the meat is cooked through, 2 minutes per side. Once cooked, place the chicken onto a paper towel–lined plate and sprinkle lightly with additional salt.

Serve with ranch, hot sauce, or mustard for dipping.

Paleo
Whole30
Gluten-Free
Dairy-Free

# Honey Chipotle Roasted Chickpeas

Serves 2

1 (15-ounce) can chickpeas, drained, rinsed, and skins removed (see Tip)

1 tablespoon honey

2 teaspoons extra-light-tasting olive oil (I like Bel'Olio)

½ teaspoon salt

¼ teaspoon ground chipotle

Recently, roasted chickpeas have started showing up in snack aisles in grocery stores everywhere. However, with a high price point for a small bag, I can't always justify buying them when they are so easy and economical to make at home. While the chickpeas we are familiar with are typically soft and tender, roasting them up creates a crunchy, portable snack that holds a lot of flavor.

Lay the rinsed chickpeas on several sheets of paper towels and set aside for about 1 hour to absorb any additional moisture.

Preheat the oven to 375°F. Line a large baking sheet with parchment paper.

Spread the chickpeas on the prepared baking sheet in an even layer. Bake for 45 minutes, or until golden and crispy. Remove from the oven, but keep the oven on.

Meanwhile, in a medium bowl, whisk together the honey, olive oil, salt, and chipotle. Add the roasted chickpeas and toss to coat.

Return the coated chickpeas to the same baking sheet and arrange them in an even layer. Bake for 5 to 7 minutes more. Let cool for 15 minutes prior to serving. Store in an airtight container up to 5 days.

**Tip** *To remove the skins from the chickpeas, place them between two paper towels and rub gently. The skins will come right off.*

Gluten-Free

Vegan

Vegetarian

Dairy-Free

Nut-Free

# Buffalo Chicken
# Sweet Potato Bites

Serves 4 to 6

**For the sweet potatoes:**

2 large sweet potatoes, sliced crosswise into ¼-inch-thick discs

1 tablespoon extra-virgin olive oil

½ teaspoon salt

⅛ teaspoon freshly ground black pepper

**For the chicken salad:**

3 cups shredded cooked chicken (dark and light meat)

½ cup 1-Minute Mayonnaise (page 195)

2 celery stalks, chopped

¼ cup Frank's RedHot hot sauce, plus more for serving

½ teaspoon salt

½ cup Dairy-Free Magic Ranch (page 207), for serving

Did you know I didn't taste my first chicken wing until I'd already graduated from college? I grew up eating boneless, skinless chicken breasts, so the idea of eating anything off the bone with the skin attached repulsed me. At the ripe age of twenty-three, I was training for my first job in Rochester, New York, when everyone went out to "the best wing place on the East Coast." I didn't want to be the loser who missed out, so off I went, planning to order whatever "boneless" wings they had on the menu. When, alas, they didn't have any, I begrudgingly ordered the regular ol' wings, and shocker: I loved them. There's something about the spicy vinegar flavor of the sauce mixed with the coolness of the dressing and celery that calls my name every time. This recipe ties all those flavors into one easy-to-make package.

**For the sweet potatoes:** Preheat the oven to 425°F. Line two large baking sheets with parchment paper.

In a medium bowl, combine the sweet potatoes, olive oil, salt, and pepper and toss to coat. Place the sweet potatoes in an even layer on the prepared baking sheets and roast for 20 minutes. Using tongs, flip the potatoes and roast for 15 to 20 minutes more, until the discs have lightly crisped and the edges are golden.

**Meanwhile, for the chicken salad:** In a large bowl, thoroughly combine the chicken, mayonnaise, celery, hot sauce, and salt.

**To assemble:** Spoon 2 tablespoons of the chicken salad onto each sweet potato disc. Drizzle with the ranch and additional hot sauce and serve.

Paleo

Whole30

Gluten-Free

Dairy-Free

Nut-Free

# Cool-er Ranch Plantains

Serves 4 to 6

1 tablespoon chili con carne seasoning or your favorite Mexican spice blend

1 tablespoon dried parsley

1 tablespoon salt

1 teaspoon lime zest

1 teaspoon garlic powder

1 teaspoon onion powder

1 teaspoon onion granules

¾ cup coconut oil

5 plantains, peeled and cut into ½-inch-thick round slices

½ cup Chipotle Crema (page 208), for serving

I think it's safe to say we've all dipped into a giant bag of our favorite party chip at some point or another, only to quickly find that we've eaten far more than the recommended serving size. I mean, when it comes to chips, does anyone really stick to that? Chips are a bottomless pit! With this recipe, I clean up the ingredients and use fried plantains in place of store-bought corn chips. The results are a perfect party treat that will actually leave you satisfied.

I recommend serving them alongside my Chipotle Crema or Cilantro Guacamole (page 211).

In a small bowl, combine the chili con carne seasoning, dried parsley, salt, lime zest, garlic powder, onion powder, and onion granules. Set aside.

In a large skillet over medium heat, melt the coconut oil. Working in batches, carefully arrange the plantain slices in a single layer in the pan and cook for 1 to 2 minutes on each side. Use a slotted spoon to transfer them to a paper towel–lined plate or cutting board. Use a mallet or the bottom of a heavy pan to flatten the slices.

Return the plantains to the pan and cook over medium heat for another minute on each side. Remove them from the oil and drain them on the plate or cutting board, lined with clean paper towels.

Sprinkle generously with the spice blend and serve with the Chipotle Crema alongside.

**Note** These plantains are double-fried. That means you pan-fry them once to soften them and then a second time after you smash them to crisp them up.

Paleo
Whole30
Gluten-Free
Dairy-Free
Nut-Free

# White Bean + Cauliflower Dip

Serves 4

2½ cups cauliflower florets

1 (15-ounce) can chickpeas, drained and rinsed (see Note)

⅓ cup extra-virgin olive oil, plus more for serving

3 garlic cloves

1 tablespoon fresh lemon juice

1¼ teaspoons salt

½ teaspoon lemon pepper, plus more for serving

I'm a sucker for throwing vegetables in wherever I can—dips and "party food" included. I love serving this dip with fresh veggies, but it's equally delicious paired with plantain chips or smeared on a slice of toast.

Fill a medium stockpot with 4 inches of water and bring to a boil.

Place a steamer basket in the stockpot and add the cauliflower florets. Steam until the cauliflower is tender but not soggy, 5 to 6 minutes. Set aside to cool for about 10 minutes.

In a blender or a food processor, combine the cooled cauliflower, chickpeas, olive oil, garlic, lemon juice, salt, and lemon pepper. Pulse until the mixture is well combined but not perfectly smooth—you want a little texture to the dip.

Refrigerate for at least 1 hour before serving. Garnish with a drizzle of olive oil and an extra dash of lemon pepper.

**Note** — *To modify for Whole30, swap out the chickpeas for 1½ cups cubed roasted white potatoes.*

Whole30-Compliant If Modified

Gluten-Free

Nut-Free

Dairy-Free

# Mac Attack Sliders with Sweet Potato Buns

## Serves 4

**For the sliders:**

2 large sweet potatoes, peeled and sliced into ½-inch-wide discs

1 tablespoon plus 2 teaspoons extra-virgin olive oil

1 teaspoon salt

½ teaspoon freshly ground black pepper

1 pound 80% lean ground beef

**For the super-special sauce:**

½ cup 1-Minute Mayonnaise (page 195)

1 tablespoon tomato paste

1 tablespoon sweet pickle relish

1 teaspoon white wine vinegar

1 teaspoon honey

½ teaspoon finely chopped white onion

¼ teaspoon coconut aminos

¼ teaspoon fish sauce

½ teaspoon salt

**To assemble:**

½ cup shredded iceberg lettuce

¼ cup finely chopped white onion (about ¼ medium)

24 dill pickle slices

Who needs a bogus trip through the drive-through when you can make these wholesome burger bites at home? 'Nuff said. Try to find the chunkiest, widest sweet potatoes possible so you can make some decent-size sliders. Bigger is definitely better in this case.

**For the sliders:** Preheat the oven to 425°F. Line two large baking sheets with parchment paper.

Place the sweet potato slices in a large bowl and toss with 1 tablespoon of the olive oil, ½ teaspoon of the salt, and ¼ teaspoon of the pepper to coat. Spread the slices in an even layer on the prepared baking sheets, being careful not to crowd them—you don't want them to steam. Roast for 20 minutes, then flip the slices over and roast for 10 to 15 minutes more, until the sweet potatoes are golden brown.

While the sweet potatoes are in the oven, in a medium bowl, combine the ground beef with the remaining ½ teaspoon salt and ¼ teaspoon pepper and mix well. Form the meat mixture into 12 small slider patties, using 2 tablespoons for each patty.

In a large skillet over medium heat, heat the remaining 2 teaspoons oil. Place the beef patties in the pan and cook for 2 to 3 minutes per side, until browned outside but still slightly pink inside.

**For the super-special sauce:** In a small bowl, combine the mayonnaise, tomato paste, relish, vinegar, honey, onion, coconut aminos, fish sauce, and salt and mix to combine.

**To assemble the sliders:** Layer a sweet potato slice with 1 teaspoon of the sauce, a pinch each of the shredded lettuce and chopped onion, a beef patty, additional sauce, and 2 pickle slices. Top with a second sweet potato disc. Repeat to make 12 sliders, and serve.

 **Note** *To modify for Whole30, omit the sweet pickle relish and honey from the sauce.*

Paleo

Whole30-Compliant If Modified

Gluten-Free

Dairy-Free

Nut-Free

# Potato Wedges with Chorizo + Poblano Peppers

2 pounds Yukon Gold potatoes, sliced into wedges (about 8 medium potatoes)

1 tablespoon plus 2 teaspoons extra-virgin olive oil

1¼ teaspoons salt

⅛ teaspoon freshly ground black pepper

1 cup chopped sweet onion (about 1 medium)

½ pound fresh chorizo (see Note)

**For the cilantro cream sauce:**

½ cup 1-Minute Mayonnaise (page 195)

⅓ cup chopped fresh cilantro

1 tablespoon unsweetened almond milk

1½ teaspoons fresh lime juice

½ teaspoon salt

**To assemble:**

⅓ cup salsa

1 small fresh poblano pepper, thinly sliced

1 medium Hass avocado, diced

1 tablespoon chopped fresh cilantro

We love football Sundays at our house . . . and all the food that goes along with it. We often invite friends over to join us and get our grub on, because isn't that half the fun?

Dishes like this are perfect for such occasions, when we're trying to keep our diets clean but still want to serve our guests something they'll enjoy. These potato wedges are so tasty and satisfying that no one will even notice they're good for you.

Preheat the oven to 425°F. Line two large baking sheets with parchment paper.

In a large bowl, toss together the potato wedges, 1 tablespoon of the olive oil, 1 teaspoon of the salt, and the black pepper until the potatoes are well coated. Spread the potatoes over the prepared baking sheets in an even layer. Roast for 20 minutes. Flip the potatoes and roast for 15 minutes more, or until the potatoes are golden brown and crisped.

In a large skillet over medium heat, heat 1 teaspoon of the oil. Add the onion and remaining ¼ teaspoon salt. Cook, stirring, until the onion is translucent and lightly browned, 5 to 6 minutes. Remove from the heat and set aside.

In the same pan, heat the remaining 1 teaspoon olive oil. Add the chorizo and cook, gently breaking the chorizo apart with a wooden spoon, until cooked through, 4 to 5 minutes.

**For the cilantro cream sauce:** In a small bowl, stir together the mayonnaise, cilantro, almond milk, lime juice, and salt.

**To assemble:** On a large plate, layer the potato wedges, chorizo, onion, salsa, poblano pepper, avocado, and cilantro cream sauce. Repeat for each serving. Garnish with the chopped cilantro and serve.

> **Note** *You can find Whole30-compliant chorizo at the meat counter at Whole Foods, or ask your butcher. In the case that you cannot find compliant chorizo, feel free to use ground pork in its place.*

Whole30
Gluten-Free
Dairy-Free
Nut-Free

# BBQ Chicken Meatballs

Serves 4 to 6

1 pound 90% lean ground chicken

½ cup grated smoked
mozzarella cheese

½ cup crushed pork rinds

¼ cup finely chopped red onion
(about ¼ medium)

1 large egg

2 garlic cloves, minced

2 tablespoons chopped fresh cilantro

½ teaspoon salt

¼ teaspoon freshly ground
black pepper

¼ teaspoon smoked paprika

2 tablespoons extra-virgin
olive or avocado oil

¼ cup barbecue sauce

One of my favorite gluten-free hacks is to use crushed pork rinds in lieu of bread crumbs in my meatballs. Not only do the rinds mimic the consistency and texture of traditional bread crumbs, but they lend much richer flavor. Plus, they're more fun to snack on while you're making the recipe!

In a large bowl, use your hands to combine the ground chicken, mozzarella, pork rinds, onion, egg, garlic, 1 tablespoon of the cilantro, the salt, pepper, and paprika.

Scoop 1 tablespoon of the meatball mixture into your hands and roll it into a 1½-inch ball. Set aside on a plate and repeat with the remaining meatball mixture.

In a large cast-iron skillet over medium heat, heat the olive oil. Working in batches to keep from overcrowding the skillet, place the meatballs in the pan, spacing them about 2 inches from one another. Fry until browned all over and cooked through, about 6 minutes total. Transfer the meatballs to a paper towel–lined plate.

When you've cooked all the meatballs, turn off the heat and drain the oil from the skillet. Return the meatballs to the pan over medium heat. Add the barbecue sauce and toss to coat; heat through for an additional 3 to 4 minutes.

Serve with the remaining 1 tablespoon cilantro sprinkled on top.

Gluten-Free

Nut-Free

# Charred Shishito Peppers + Sriracha Dip

Serves 4

**For the Sriracha dip:**

½ cup 1-Minute Mayonnaise
(page 195)

1 tablespoon Sriracha

1 garlic clove, minced

½ teaspoon fresh lime juice

½ teaspoon coconut aminos

⅛ teaspoon salt

**For the shishito peppers:**

2 teaspoons avocado oil

¼ teaspoon toasted sesame oil

2 pounds shishito peppers

1 to 2 tablespoons flaky sea salt
(I like Maldon)

I'm trying to figure out how to illustrate just how tasty these darn little peppers are. Perhaps the fact that my husband and I eat them up ourselves in all of three minutes is enough? If you're looking for a crazy-easy appetizer to make in a short amount of time, this is it. It's perfect for game nights, football Sundays, whatever!

**For the Sriracha dip:** In a small bowl, thoroughly combine the mayonnaise, Sriracha, garlic, lime juice, coconut aminos, and salt. Set aside.

**For the shishito peppers:** In a large cast-iron skillet over medium-high heat, heat the avocado oil and sesame oil. Add the shishito peppers and cook, turning occasionally, until they are lightly charred and softened, 4 to 5 minutes.

Sprinkle the sea salt over the peppers and serve with the Sriracha dip alongside.

> **Note** *To modify for Whole30, swap out the Sriracha for a compliant hot sauce, such as Frank's RedHot, Tabasco, or Yai's Thai Chili Garlic Hot Sauce.*

Paleo

Whole30-
Compliant If
Modified

Gluten-Free

Vegetarian

Dairy-Free

Nut-Free

# Chimichurri Party Wings

**Serves 4 to 6**

3 teaspoons salt

¼ teaspoon freshly ground black pepper

2 pounds chicken wings, tips removed and separated at the joint into 2 pieces

½ cup extra-virgin olive oil

⅓ cup chopped fresh cilantro

¼ cup chopped fresh parsley

1 teaspoon lime zest (from about 1 lime)

2 tablespoons fresh lime juice (from about 2 limes)

1 tablespoon honey (see Note)

½ teaspoon ground cumin

½ teaspoon chili powder

¼ teaspoon red pepper flakes

After I perfected these wings, I just knew they were going to be one of the most popular recipes in this book, because they are *just* that delicious and easy to make. In fact, my dear friend Teresa said she'd buy my book just for this recipe (as did my totally unbiased mom and husband). These are a surefire hit.

Preheat the oven to 450°F. Line two large baking sheets with parchment paper.

Sprinkle 1 teaspoon of the salt and the black pepper over the chicken wings and set aside.

In a large bowl, combine the olive oil, cilantro, parsley, lime zest, lime juice, honey, cumin, chili powder, red pepper flakes, and remaining 2 teaspoons salt and stir until the honey has dissolved. Set aside about one-third of the chimichurri for serving.

Add the wings to the bowl with the remaining chimichurri and toss to coat well.

Place the coated chicken wings on the prepared baking sheets, evenly spaced apart. Roast for 20 minutes. Using tongs, flip the wings and roast for 15 minutes more, until some of the edges are charred and the meat is cooked through.

Transfer to a serving platter. Brush the reserved chimichurri over the wings and serve.

**Note**   *To modify for Whole30, omit the honey.*

Paleo

Whole30-Compliant If Modified

Gluten-Free

Dairy-Free

Nut-Free

# Tzatziki Dip

Serves 4

1 cup 1-Minute Mayonnaise
(page 195)

2 tablespoons chopped fresh dill

1½ tablespoons unsweetened
almond milk or full-fat coconut milk

1 garlic clove, minced

½ teaspoon grated lemon zest

½ teaspoon salt

Extra-virgin olive oil, for drizzling

Freshly ground black pepper,
for serving

When I first changed up my diet, I had no clue what you could pair with dip other than bread and chips. Turns out: a lot! This dip is particularly great with bell peppers, cucumbers, and even the lamb meatballs from my Mediterranean Bowls (page 80). If you're not a big dipper, feel free to serve this on top of some freshly grilled fish!

In a medium bowl, stir together the mayonnaise, dill, almond milk, garlic, lemon zest, and salt until well combined.

Serve topped with a drizzle of olive oil and a crack of black pepper.

Paleo
Whole30
Gluten-Free
Vegetarian
Dairy-Free
Nut-Free

# Lunchtime

# Spicy Tuna–Stuffed Bell Peppers

1 (5-ounce) can albacore tuna packed in water, drained

¼ cup 1-Minute Mayonnaise (page 195)

1 scallion, sliced

1 tablespoon hot sauce

½ teaspoon coconut aminos

¼ teaspoon rice vinegar

1 red bell pepper, halved lengthwise

½ medium cucumber, thinly sliced

1 medium Hass avocado, thinly sliced

⅛ teaspoon sesame seeds, toasted (see Tip, page 111)

This has got to be one of my favorite lunches. Is it a sandwich? Is it sushi? Okay, it's not sushi, but who knows? What I *can* tell you is that it's delicious. Screw the bread and seaweed—this sandwich/sushi/whatever comes delivered in a hollowed-out pepper. And it rocks. Not only that, but this stuffed pepper—filled to replicate the flavors of a spicy tuna roll—will satisfy any sushi craving, because, really, who has the time and coordination to make sushi at home? Certainly not I. To top it all off (and because I love tinkering with and adding extra nutrients to things), I bring this baby home with some cucumber and avocado.

In a small bowl, combine the tuna, mayonnaise, scallion, hot sauce, coconut aminos, and vinegar.

Line each pepper cavity with half of the cucumber and avocado slices, then fill with half of the tuna. Sprinkle with the toasted sesame seeds and serve.

Paleo

Whole30

Gluten-Free

Dairy-Free

Nut-Free

# Green Goddess Wrap

**Serves 2**

4 large rainbow chard leaves, stems and inner ribs removed

½ medium cucumber, thinly sliced

1 medium Hass avocado, sliced

1 cup sprouts or microgreens

[⅔] cup shredded cooked chicken (light and dark meat)

½ cup pepperoncini

½ cup Dairy-Free Green Goddess Dressing (page 213)

2 tablespoons crumbled goat cheese (optional; see Note)

Pinch of salt

This is one of those recipes that's perfect to prep ahead of time. There's nothing better than opening your fridge and finding your lunch laid out in front of you with only a bit of assembly required. Word to the wise: This recipe *can* get a bit messy to eat. But that's what napkins are for, right? If you're planning to pack this up for work, I suggest chopping the chard into bite-size pieces and turning this recipe into a salad to make it a bit neater, since we all know that the grumpy HR lady isn't going to tell you if you have a giant glob of avocado and dressing on your chin.

On a cutting board, lay 2 pieces of the rainbow chard on top of each other. (I like to invert them so that I have even layers.) Lay half of the cucumber slices lengthwise over the chard. Top with half of the avocado slices and sprouts, then layer with half of the chicken and pepperoncini. Drizzle with ¼ cup of the Green Goddess and top with 1 tablespoon of the crumbled goat cheese and a sprinkle of salt.

 Working lengthwise, slowly and tightly roll up the chard leaves around the filling, being careful not to tear the chard. Repeat to make the second wrap. Slice the rolls in half and serve.

**Note** *To modify for Whole30 and to make dairy-free, omit the goat cheese.*

Paleo

Whole30-Compliant If Modified

Gluten-Free

Dairy-Free

Nut-Free

# Harissa Chicken Salad

**Serves 4**

2 cups shredded rotisserie chicken

1 red bell pepper, chopped

½ cup chopped red onion
(about ½ medium)

½ cup canned chickpeas, drained
and rinsed (see Note)

½ cup 1-Minute Mayonnaise
(page 195)

¼ cup harissa (I like Mina)

3 tablespoons chopped fresh cilantro

1 teaspoon salt

¼ cup sliced almonds

8 cups baby spinach

If you've yet to try harissa, you are missing out, my friend. It's a spicy sauce or paste made with a blend of ingredients like chile peppers, garlic, cumin, and coriander and used frequently in Middle Eastern and North African cooking. It's sure to elevate any dish you add it to, and this chicken salad is no exception. If you love heat like I do, add an extra tablespoon of harissa to this recipe.

In a large bowl, combine the chicken, bell pepper, onion, chickpeas, mayonnaise, harissa, cilantro, and salt and stir to combine. Fold in the sliced almonds.

Divide the baby spinach among six plates and top each with a scoop of chicken salad.

 Note ▶ *To modify for Whole30, omit the chickpeas and use 1 cup chopped celery instead.*

Paleo

Whole30-
Compliant If
Modified

Dairy-Free

Gluten-Free

# Brussels Salad

Serves 2 to 4

6 cups shredded Brussels sprouts
(about 1 pound)

8 dates, pitted and cut into
bite-size pieces

⅓ cup freshly grated Pecorino
Romano cheese

3 tablespoons pepitas
(pumpkin seeds)

¼ teaspoon salt

Mustard-Maple Vinaigrette
(page 203)

6 hard-boiled large eggs, sliced,
for serving

Freshly ground black pepper

Twenty years ago, nobody would have thought to use raw Brussels sprouts in a salad. Back then, Brussels sprouts were the most dreaded of all veggies, known only as brown, soggy, bitter monstrosities. Kids around the world loathed them, and they were the butt of every veggie joke out there. Fast-forward to today, we finally figured out how to do them justice and can't get enough of 'em! Whether they're fried, roasted, or raw, Brussels sprouts are the vegetable kingdom's ultimate comeback kid.

In a large bowl, combine the Brussels sprouts, dates, cheese, and pepitas. Sprinkle with the salt and toss with vinaigrette to taste. Top with the sliced eggs and season with pepper.

Gluten-Free
Vegetarian
Nut-Free

## Serves 4 to 6

1½ cups green lentils, rinsed

2 medium tomatoes, diced

⅓ cup chopped red onion
(about ⅓ medium)

¼ cup chopped fresh basil

2 garlic cloves, minced

1 tablespoon extra-virgin olive oil

1 teaspoon salt

# Bruschetta Lentils

For years, I purchased a dish similar to this one at a local supermarket. But once I started making it at home for a fraction of the price, there was no turning back. Lentils are quite easy to prepare ahead of time, and they hold up great throughout the week for leftovers, making them a good option for meal prepping and on-the-go lunching. Add a bit of Pecorino Romano or goat cheese for an extra dimension of flavor. (Note that adding the cheese will make this dish inherently un-dairy-free and un-vegan. So don't serve it that way to your vegan buddies. And yes, those are official terms.)

In a large saucepan, combine the lentils and 3 cups of water and bring to a boil. Reduce the heat to medium-low, bring to a low simmer, and cover the pot. Cook for 15 to 20 minutes, until the lentils are tender but not mushy. Drain the lentils, transfer to a large bowl, and let cool to room temperature.

Add the tomatoes, onion, basil, garlic, olive oil, and salt and stir to combine. Refrigerate for at least 1 hour prior to serving.

Gluten-Free

Vegan

Vegetarian

Dairy-Free

Nut-Free

GREAT FOR
LEFTOVERS!
★ ★ ★

## Serves 2 to 4

2 (6-ounce) cans salmon packed
in water, drained

½ medium cucumber, seeded
and cut into bite-size pieces

½ cup 1-Minute Mayonnaise
(page 195)

¼ cup chopped red onion
(about ¼ medium)

2 tablespoons chopped fresh dill

1 tablespoon whole-grain mustard

½ teaspoon salt

¼ teaspoon lemon pepper

1 medium Hass avocado, diced

½ grapefruit, peeled, pith removed,
and cut into ¼-inch segments

Your favorite greens, for serving
(optional)

Paleo

Whole30

Gluten-Free

Dairy-Free

Nut-Free

# Salmon-Avocado Salad

Step aside, tuna salad! We have a new friend in
town: salmon salad. And she's amazing. I use
canned salmon for this recipe to keep it convenient
for lunches, but you can always substitute cooked
fresh salmon.

In a large bowl, combine the salmon, cucumber, mayonnaise, onion, dill,
mustard, salt, and lemon pepper and toss. Gently fold in the avocado and
grapefruit.

Serve on its own or over a bed of your favorite greens.

# Chickpea-Avocado Sando

Serves 4

**For the chickpea-avocado salad:**

1 cup canned chickpeas,
drained and rinsed

1½ tablespoons extra-virgin olive oil

½ teaspoon salt

⅛ teaspoon freshly ground
black pepper or lemon pepper

⅛ teaspoon red pepper flakes

1 medium Hass avocado

**For the garlic aioli:**

¼ cup 1-Minute Mayonnaise
(page 195)

2 garlic cloves, minced

Salt and freshly ground black pepper
or lemon pepper

**To assemble:**

8 slices bread (I like gluten-free
Canyon Bakehouse)

1 cup loosely packed baby spinach

½ cup microgreens or sprouts

I used to love me some sandwiches back in the day. In fact, I probably ate one every day. I'd load a giant hunk of Dutch crunch or sourdough with turkey, lettuce, extra cheese, and extra pickles. Some sandwich.

Times have changed, so while I don't have a sandwich every day, I do enjoy one from time to time. I've learned how to clean them up a bit and add some extra nutrients with things like spinach and sprouts, because pickles don't count as a vegetable, no matter how many you add. If you want to skip the bread altogether, pile your sandwich fixings into to a hollowed-out bell pepper or on top of cucumber slices.

**For the chickpea-avocado salad:** In a blender or food processor, combine the chickpeas, olive oil, salt, black pepper, and red pepper flakes and pulse four or five times, until the chickpeas are chopped but not smooth. Scrape the chickpea mixture into a small bowl and add the avocado. Mash the mixture together with a fork. Set aside.

**For the garlic aioli:** In a small bowl, combine the mayonnaise and garlic. Season with salt and black pepper.

**To assemble:** Spread the aioli over each slice of bread, dividing it evenly. Load 4 slices of the bread with ¼ cup of the spinach and 2 tablespoons of the microgreens. Divide ¼ of the chickpea-avocado salad over the greens and top with a second piece of bread, aioli-side down. Serve immediately. Refrigerate any remaining chickpea-avocado salad for up to 3 days.

Gluten-Free

Vegetarian

Dairy-Free

Nut-Free

# Egg Salad Cucumber Boats

**Serves 4 to 6**

8 large eggs

⅓ cup 1-Minute Mayonnaise (page 195)

1 celery stalk, chopped

2 tablespoons dill pickle relish (make sure it's sugar- and dye-free)

1 tablespoon Dijon mustard

1 tablespoon chopped fresh dill

1 teaspoon salt, plus more as needed

2 large cucumbers, halved lengthwise and seeds scooped out

2 medium tomatoes, sliced (I like heirlooms here, but any variety will do)

A few things my husband, Brad, and I don't see eye-to-eye on: hip-hop (he is *not* a fan), the fact that the toilet paper is supposed to fold over the *top* of the roll, and egg salad. Yes, egg salad. Now, my husband is one of the least picky eaters I've ever met—he likes tripe, liver, menudo, and almost any other adventurous thing you can think of—but he won't touch a hard-boiled egg. It grosses him out. Which is crazy to me because I love any form of hard-boiled egg, from deviled eggs to this egg salad–loaded cucumber boat. Brad is missing out!

Fill a stockpot with 4 inches of water. Set a steamer basket above the water and bring the water to a boil. Put the eggs in the steamer basket, cover, and cook for 10 to 11 minutes. Transfer the eggs to a bowl of ice water and let cool for 10 minutes, then drain. Peel and chop the eggs.

In a large bowl, stir together the chopped eggs, mayonnaise, celery, relish, mustard, dill, and salt.

Halve the cucumber halves crosswise and line the cavities with the tomato slices. Scoop the egg salad over the tomatoes and season with salt. Serve immediately.

Paleo
Whole30
Vegetarian
Gluten-Free
Dairy-Free
Nut-Free

# Mediterranean Bowls

When it comes to meal prep and planning, this recipe's got you covered. The components are all easy to make ahead in batches, so you can portion them out for easy lunches all week.

**Serves 4**

**For the dressing:**

¼ cup extra-virgin olive oil

1 tablespoon white wine vinegar

1 teaspoon fresh lemon juice

½ teaspoon salt

**For the meatballs:**

1 pound ground lamb

¼ cup finely chopped red onion (about ¼ medium)

2 garlic cloves, minced

1 tablespoon chopped fresh parsley, plus more for serving

1 tablespoon chopped fresh mint

1 teaspoon fresh lemon juice

1 teaspoon salt

½ teaspoon ground cumin

½ teaspoon ground cinnamon

1 tablespoon extra-virgin olive oil

**For the cauliflower rice:**

1 small head cauliflower, cut into florets, or 4 cups store-bought cauliflower rice

1 tablespoon extra-virgin olive oil

½ teaspoon lemon pepper

½ teaspoon salt

**To assemble:**

1 red bell pepper, sliced

1 cup pitted kalamata olives

1 cup marinated artichoke hearts

**For the dressing:** In a medium bowl, whisk together the olive oil, vinegar, and lemon juice. Season with the salt and set aside.

**For the meatballs:** In a large bowl, use your hands to thoroughly combine the lamb, onion, garlic, parsley, mint, lemon juice, salt, cumin, and cinnamon. Shape the lamb mixture into 16 meatballs, using about 1½ tablespoons for each.

In a large skillet over medium heat, heat the olive oil. Working in batches so you don't crowd the pan, add the meatballs and cook until cooked through and golden brown all over, 10 to 12 minutes total.

**For the cauliflower rice:** If using fresh cauliflower, in a food processor, pulse the cauliflower florets until broken down to a rice-like consistency. (Skip this step if using store-bought cauliflower rice.)

In a clean large skillet over medium heat, heat the olive oil. Add the cauliflower rice, lemon pepper, and salt. Stir in ¼ cup water and cook until the cauliflower is tender but not mushy, 6 to 7 minutes.

**To assemble:** Into each bowl, scoop ½ cup of the cauliflower rice. Top with one-quarter each of the bell pepper, olives, and artichoke hearts, 4 of the meatballs, and a drizzle of the dressing. Garnish each with a pinch of parsley and serve.

Paleo

Whole30

Gluten-Free

Dairy-Free

Nut-Free

# Mexican Slaw

Serves 4

**For the dressing:**

¼ cup extra-virgin olive oil

2 tablespoons fresh lime juice

1 teaspoon honey

1 garlic clove, minced

½ teaspoon salt

**To assemble:**

4 cups coleslaw mix

1 red bell pepper, chopped

¼ cup chopped fresh cilantro

3 tablespoons pepitas
(pumpkin seeds)

6 hard-boiled large eggs
(see page 79), peeled and chopped

⅓ cup crushed store-bought
plantain chips

One of the things I love about a good slaw is how well it holds up, which makes it a perfect make-ahead dish. Whether it's for lunch or to bring to a potluck, cabbage is so much heartier than the lettuce or spinach when used in traditional salads, so dressing it ahead of time is no big deal. Feel free to throw some shredded chicken or grilled shrimp onto this dish for some additional protein.

**For the dressing:** In a small bowl, whisk together the olive oil, lime juice, honey, garlic, and salt until emulsified.

   **To assemble:** In a large bowl, combine the coleslaw mix, bell pepper, cilantro, and pepitas and toss with the dressing. Top with the chopped egg and plantain chips and serve.

 Note    *To modify for Whole30, omit the honey and plantain chips.*

Paleo

Whole30-
Compliant If
Modified

Gluten-Free

Vegetarian

Dairy-Free

Nut-Free

# Peach + Prosciutto Salad

Serves 4

3 tablespoons extra-virgin olive oil

1 tablespoon champagne vinegar

2 teaspoons honey

½ teaspoon salt

6 cups packed baby spinach

2 cups packed watercress

½ cup Marcona almonds

½ cup fresh blueberries

⅓ cup crumbled blue cheese

8 slices prosciutto, halved

2 peaches, sliced

What's not to love about this salad? Fresh peaches? Check. Prosciutto? Check. Combined with some blue cheese? Trust me, you're in for a treat.

In a small bowl, whisk together the olive oil, vinegar, honey, and salt until emulsified.

In a large bowl, toss together the spinach, watercress, almonds, blue-berries, and blue cheese. Add the dressing and toss to coat. Garnish the salad with the prosciutto and peach slices and serve.

Gluten-Free

# Spiralized Beet Salad

Serves 4

2 medium beets, peeled and spiralized using a large blade

¼ cup plus ½ teaspoon extra-virgin olive oil

2 shallots, thinly sliced

1 tablespoon Dijon mustard

1½ teaspoons balsamic vinegar

⅛ teaspoon salt

6 cups arugula

2 medium oranges, peeled and cut into ¼-inch segments

⅓ cup roasted hazelnuts

¼ cup crumbled goat cheese (see Note)

While beets may be one of the tastiest vegetables to spiralize, they're also one of the messiest. Don't be scared—I just suggest you don't wear white while you're prepping them. Actually, now that I think about it, wear black. All black. Head to toe. You can thank me later. Beets are such a great way to add nutrients to your diet, the sartorial sacrifice will be worth it.

Preheat the oven to 400°F. Line a large baking sheet with parchment paper.

In a large bowl, toss the spiralized beets with ¼ teaspoon of the olive oil. Spread the beets evenly over the prepared baking sheet and roast for 5 to 7 minutes, until the beets are slightly tender. Set aside.

In a small skillet over medium heat, heat ¼ teaspoon of the oil. Add the shallots and cook, stirring, until they are tender and the edges are lightly browned, 3 to 4 minutes. Remove the pan from the heat and set aside.

In a small bowl, whisk together the remaining ¼ cup olive oil, the mustard, vinegar, and salt.

In a large serving bowl, combine the arugula, oranges, hazelnuts, and goat cheese. Add two-thirds of the dressing and toss to coat. Tuft the crisped beets on top and drizzle with the remaining salad dressing. Serve.

**Note** *To modify for Whole30, omit the goat cheese.*

Paleo

Whole30-Compliant If Modified

Gluten-Free

Vegetarian

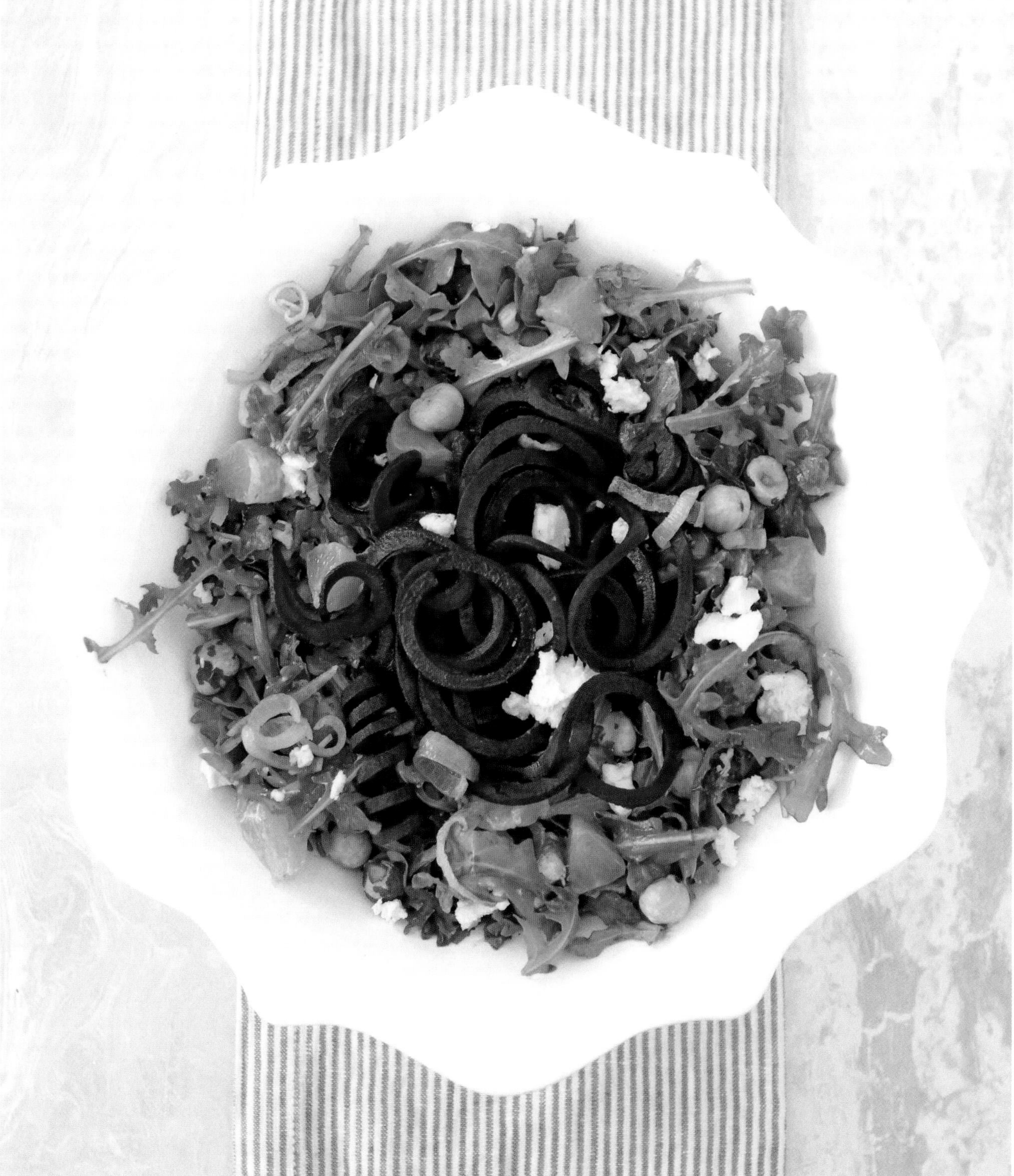

# Vietnamese-Style Lettuce Wraps

### Serves 4 to 6

**For the sauce:**

¼ cup extra-light-tasting olive or avocado oil (I like Bel'Olio)

4 teaspoons fish sauce

2 teaspoons fresh lime juice

2 teaspoons Sriracha or chili sauce

2 teaspoons rice vinegar

1 teaspoon honey (see Note)

2 garlic cloves, minced

½ teaspoon finely grated fresh ginger

**To assemble:**

8 whole butter or Bibb lettuce leaves

2 cups shredded cooked chicken (dark and light meat)

1 medium carrot, grated

1 red bell pepper, thinly sliced

1 medium Hass avocado, sliced

1 cup snow peas

1 cup mung bean sprouts

8 fresh mint leaves

⅓ cup fresh cilantro leaves

This is one of those recipes that screams "food-prep me!" If you prep the ingredients ahead of time and store them in airtight containers in the fridge, you'll have an easy-to-make lunch all week long.

**For the sauce:** In a small bowl, whisk together the olive oil, fish sauce, lime juice, Sriracha, vinegar, honey, garlic, and ginger. Set aside.

**To assemble:** Lay 1 lettuce leaf flat on a cutting board. Add ¼ cup of the chicken along the middle of the lettuce leaf and continue to layer with approximately one-eighth of each of the remaining ingredients. Repeat until you've assembled 8 wraps.

 Note *To modify for Whole30, omit the honey from the sauce, and check the ingredients in your Sriracha or chili sauce.*

Paleo

Whole30-Compliant If Modified

Gluten-Free

Dairy-Free

Nut-Free

# Dinner

# The Whole Smiths' Whole Roasted Chicken

### Serves 4 to 6

2 pounds carrots, halved lengthwise

½ medium sweet onion, quartered

4 garlic cloves, smashed

3 tablespoons extra-virgin olive oil

1 teaspoon salt

1 (4-pound) whole chicken

1½ teaspoons lemon pepper

1 teaspoon extra-flaky sea salt
(I like Maldon)

I'm not sure why, but for the longest time, I was intimidated by roasting a whole chicken. I thought there was some fancy advanced culinary technique to it, but I was dead wrong. This recipe is something even the most novice of cooks can master. It's quickly become one of the most popular recipes on my blog, and for good reason. It's a breeze to whip up, it provides you with leftovers for lunch the next day (see the Harissa Chicken Salad on page 68), and you can use the leftover bones for broth. It's the gift that keeps on giving.

Preheat the oven to 450°F.

In a large bowl, combine the carrots, onion, garlic, 2 tablespoons of the olive oil, and the salt and toss to coat.

Transfer the vegetables to an 11 by 13-inch baking dish and place the chicken breast-side up over the vegetables.

Drizzle the remaining 1 tablespoon oil over the chicken and rub it into the skin, thoroughly coating it. Sprinkle the lemon pepper and flaky sea salt over the chicken and gently rub into the skin.

Place the baking dish on the center rack of the oven and roast for 30 minutes. Reduce the oven temperature to 425°F and roast for 45 to 60 minutes more, until the chicken has an internal temperature of 165°F. Let cool for 10 minutes prior to serving.

| Tip | *The secret to getting that desirable extra-crispy skin on a roast chicken is to loosen the skin from the flesh before dressing it. To do this, gently run your finger under the skin of the chicken before doing anything else. This creates an air pocket that will keep your chicken moist while also giving you the crispiest skin possible.* |

Paleo

Whole30

Gluten-Free

Dairy-Free

Nut-Free

# Spaghetti Squash Tuna Casserole

Serves 4 to 6

**For the cashew cream sauce:**

2 cups raw unsalted cashews, soaked in hot water for 30 minutes and drained

¼ cup unsweetened almond milk

3 garlic cloves

1 teaspoon salt

½ teaspoon garlic powder

¼ teaspoon freshly ground black pepper

¼ teaspoon ground nutmeg

**For the squash:**

1 tablespoon extra-virgin olive oil

2 medium spaghetti squash, quartered (see Note, page 155)

½ teaspoon salt

¼ teaspoon freshly ground black pepper

**To assemble:**

2 tablespoons extra-virgin olive oil, plus more for greasing

½ medium white onion, chopped (about ½ cup)

2½ teaspoons salt

8 ounces cremini mushrooms, chopped

2 (5-ounce) cans albacore tuna packed in water, drained

3 large eggs, beaten

1 cup crushed pork rinds (see Note)

While a traditional tuna casserole is one of America's favorite comfort foods, it ranks pretty low on the nutritional scale. I decided to replace some of the processed components and remove the pasta altogether for this version, which is just as creamy and satisfying. You get all the comfort and less of the junk!

Preheat the oven to 450°F.

**For the cashew cream sauce:** In a blender or food processor, combine the cashews, almond milk, garlic cloves, salt, garlic powder, pepper, nutmeg, and 1 cup water. Blend on high until smooth, about 30 seconds. Set aside.

**For the squash:** Drizzle the olive oil over the flesh of the spaghetti squash and season with the salt and pepper. Place the squash skin-side down on two large baking sheets. Roast for 30 to 35 minutes, until the squash is fork-tender and the edges have browned. Let the squash cool and reduce the oven temperature to 375°F.

**To assemble:** While the squash roasts, in a large skillet over medium heat, heat 1 tablespoon of the olive oil. Add the onion and ½ teaspoon of the salt and cook, stirring frequently, until the onion is tender and the edges have browned, 7 to 8 minutes. Transfer the onion to a large bowl and set aside.

In the same pan, heat the remaining 1 tablespoon oil. Add the mushrooms and 1 teaspoon of the salt, and cook, stirring, until they are tender and have released most of their moisture, 8 to 9 minutes. Set aside.

Once the spaghetti squash is cool enough to handle, scrape the flesh into the bowl with the cooked onion. Add the cashew cream sauce, mushrooms, tuna, beaten eggs, and remaining 1 teaspoon salt. Using your hands, combine the ingredients until they are thoroughly incorporated.

Lightly grease a 9 by 13-inch baking pan with olive oil.

Pour the spaghetti squash mixture into the prepared pan and spread it into an even layer. Bake the casserole for 40 minutes. Remove from the oven and sprinkle with the crushed pork rinds. Return to the oven and bake for 15 minutes more, or until the casserole is cooked through and the edges have browned. Slice the casserole to serve.

**Note** *To modify for Whole30, omit the pork rinds.*

Paleo

Whole30-Compliant If Modified

Gluten-Free

Dairy-Free

# Zucchini Lasagna Roll-Ups

## Serves 4 to 6

1 tablespoon extra-virgin olive oil

1 cup chopped yellow onion (about ½ medium)

2 teaspoons salt

3 garlic cloves, minced

¾ pound mild Italian sausage, casings removed (see Tip)

¾ pound 85% lean ground beef

2 cups prepared marinara sauce

2 large zucchini, sliced lengthwise into ⅛-inch-thick slices (a mandoline works well here)

1 cup ricotta cheese (see Note)

Every year, we rent a plot of land at our daughter's school where we plant our garden. Last year, we went a little crazy with the zucchini. We had so many that we were eating them for breakfast, lunch, and dinner. I think it may have traumatized the kids, because they're zucchini-phobic now and protest (loudly, heavily, and incessantly) any time they see one in the kitchen. So imagine their frustration with this recipe. When my youngest (she's five) saw me slicing the zucchini, she gave me her usual protest—"Zucchini!? NO! Not again!"—complete with a dramatic groan and sigh. Being the mean, mean mom that I am, I forced her to try it at dinner despite the scowl on her face. Ten long minutes later, she took a bite and replaced her scowl with a look of confusion and embarrassment. She liked it, but didn't know what to do about it. She took another bite, smirked, and said, "Mmm, that's pretty good!" No kidding, kid.

Preheat the oven to 375°F.

In a large sauté pan over medium heat, heat the olive oil. Add the onion and ½ teaspoon of the salt and cook, stirring frequently, until the onion is tender and translucent, 7 to 8 minutes. Add the garlic and cook, stirring frequently, until fragrant, 1 minute. Add the sausage, ground beef, and remaining 1½ teaspoons salt. Cook, stirring and using a wooden spoon to gently break up the meat as it cooks, until cooked through, 7 to 8 minutes. Stir in the marina sauce and remove from the heat.

Pour 1 cup of the meat sauce into a 10-inch round baking dish and spread it evenly over the bottom. Set aside.

Lay the zucchini slices on a flat work surface. Spoon 1 tablespoon of the meat sauce and 1 teaspoon of the ricotta on one end of each slice. Roll up the zucchini and place it in the baking dish. Repeat with the remaining zucchini. Pour additional meat sauce over the rolled zucchini in the baking dish.

Bake for 25 minutes, or until the sauce bubbles and the zucchini is tender.

**Note** To modify this for Paleo, Whole30, or to be dairy-free, I like to use a nut-based, dairy-free ricotta cheese like the one from Kite Hill.

**Tip** Make sure to check the ingredients in your sausage if you're looking to make this Whole30 compliant. If you cannot find a compliant sausage, regular ground pork will be just as tasty.

# Chipotle-Lime Shrimp

**Serves 4**

¾ cup extra-virgin olive oil

½ cup chopped fresh cilantro, plus extra for garnish

4 garlic cloves, minced

¼ cup fresh lime juice (from about 3 limes)

1 tablespoon ground chipotle

1 teaspoon salt

1 pound large raw shrimp, peeled and deveined

Grilled vegetable of your choice, for serving

These grilled shrimp kebabs just may be the best shrimp I've ever had. Truth. Serve them with some braised kale or grilled zucchini for a perfect meal, brushing any extra marinade over the veggies before braising or grilling.

In a large zip-top plastic bag, combine the olive oil, cilantro, garlic, lime juice, chipotle, and salt, seal the bag, and toss to thoroughly combine. Add the shrimp, seal the bag, and toss to coat. Set aside to marinate at room temperature for 1 hour.

Heat an outdoor grill to high or heat a grill pan over high heat.

Thread the marinated shrimp onto skewers, reserving the marinade. Grill for 3 minutes per side, brushing on the reserved marinade as they cook.

Garnish with cilantro and serve immediately with the grilled veggie of your choice.

Paleo
Whole30
Gluten-Free
Dairy-Free
Nut-Free

# Spaghetti Squash Chicken Alfredo

## Serves 4

4 boneless, skin-on chicken breasts (see Tip)

Salt and freshly ground black pepper

1 large spaghetti squash, quartered and seeded (see Note, page 155)

3 tablespoons plus 1 teaspoon extra-virgin olive oil

8 garlic cloves

1 cup cashews, soaked overnight and drained

1 tablespoon unsweetened almond milk

¼ cup chopped fresh basil, plus extra for garnish

One of the scariest things I've ever done is slice a spaghetti squash. Okay, that's an exaggeration, but do be cautious and use a sharp knife when you're working with one. And wear gloves. An eye guard may be handy, too. Just kidding, you got this! But proceed with caution. The results—crisp, fresh, noodly squash with creamy chicken—are well worth the trouble.

Preheat the oven to 425°F. Line a large baking sheet with parchment paper.

Season the chicken breasts generously with salt and pepper and set aside.

Lightly coat the cut sides of the squash with 1 tablespoon of the olive oil and sprinkle generously with salt and pepper. Place the squash skin-side down on the prepared baking sheet and set aside.

In a small bowl, lightly toss the garlic with 1 teaspoon of the olive oil. Place the garlic on the baking sheet with the spaghetti squash. Roast for 20 minutes, then remove the roasted garlic and set it aside. Roast the squash for 10 to 20 minutes more, until the edges start to brown.

In a blender, combine the roasted garlic, remaining 2 tablespoons oil, the cashews, almond milk, and 1 tablespoon water. Blend until creamy. Taste and season with salt.

Heat a grill to medium or heat a grill pan over medium heat.

Place the chicken breasts skin-side down on the grill or in the grill pan and cook until the internal temperature reaches 165°F, 5 to 6 minutes on each side.

Scrape the flesh of the spaghetti squash into a large serving bowl and toss with the cashew cream and basil.

Slice the chicken breasts and serve over the spaghetti squash garnished with basil.

**Tip** *I always get my boneless, skin-on chicken breasts from the meat counter at my local grocery store, where they are happy to remove the bones for me (or you can remove them yourself at home). While I prefer to leave the skin on, this recipe will be just as delicious if you use boneless, skinless chicken breasts.*

Paleo
Whole30
Gluten-Free
Dairy-Free

# Salmon with Creamy Dill Shredded Squash

## Serves 4

1 tablespoon lemon pepper

2 teaspoons grated lemon zest

2 teaspoons salt

4 (6-ounce) skin-on salmon fillets (about 1½ pounds)

3 medium zucchini or yellow squash or a mixture (about 1 pound), grated

⅓ cup goat cheese

1 tablespoon fresh lemon juice

⅓ cup pine nuts, toasted (see Tip)

2 tablespoons chopped fresh dill

2 teaspoons chopped fresh chives

1 tablespoon extra-virgin olive oil

Sliced lemon, for garnish (optional)

Because we have an abundance of zucchini from our garden each summer, I've had to get creative on how to prepare it. I started making this creamy, lemony shredded zucchini, and I could make this using every zucchini I ever grow for the rest of my life and never get sick of it. It's a bold statement, but it's the truth. Nothing gets better than these ingredients—fresh dill, creamy goat cheese, zesty lemon—particularly when they're paired with salmon.

In a small bowl, combine the lemon pepper, 1 teaspoon of the lemon zest, and 1 teaspoon of the salt. Sprinkle the seasoning over each side of the salmon fillets and set aside.

Fill a stockpot one-third of the way with water and bring the water to a boil. Add the grated zucchini and cook for 1 minute. Drain the zucchini in a fine-mesh strainer, gently pressing the zucchini to release as much water as possible. Return the zucchini to the pot over low heat. Stir in the goat cheese, lemon juice, remaining 1 teaspoon lemon zest, and remaining 1 teaspoon salt. Add the pine nuts, dill, and chives and gently combine. Keep warm over low heat.

In a large cast-iron skillet over medium heat, heat the olive oil. Place the salmon fillets skin-side down in the skillet and cook until the skin has crisped and the salmon is cooked about halfway through, 2 to 3 minutes. Flip the salmon and cook until seared through, 2 to 3 minutes more.

Serve each salmon fillet on a bed of the shredded zucchini. Garnish with lemon slices, if desired.

**Tip** *To toast the pine nuts, heat a small skillet over medium-low heat and spread the pine nuts into an even layer. Cook, stirring the pine nuts continuously, until they are slightly golden and toasted, about 3 minutes. Transfer to a plate and let cool.*

Gluten-Free
Nut-Free

# Broccoli Chicken Ranch Potatoes

### Serves 4 to 6

3 medium russet potatoes, scrubbed clean

1½ teaspoons extra-virgin olive oil

2 teaspoons salt

3 tablespoons ghee or salted butter

3 scallions, chopped

2 garlic cloves, minced

1½ tablespoons chopped fresh dill

1 tablespoon chopped fresh parsley

1 tablespoon nutritional yeast

2 teaspoons chopped fresh chives

¼ teaspoon freshly ground black pepper

½ pound broccoli florets (from about ½ head)

2 cups shredded cooked chicken (light and dark meat)

I really wanted to include a Whole30-compliant twice-baked potato in this book. Even though twice-baked potatoes usually have cheese (and lots of it), I decided to make a go at creating a version so loaded with flavor and goodness that nobody would even miss the extra dairy. I'm here to tell you that I succeeded.

Preheat the oven to 450°F. Line a large baking sheet with parchment paper.

Prick holes in the potatoes with a fork, then coat with the olive oil and sprinkle with 1 teaspoon of the salt. Place the potatoes on the prepared baking sheet and bake for 1 hour. Let cool. Reduce the oven temperature to 375°F.

Cut the cooled potatoes in half lengthwise and scrape the flesh into a large bowl, reserving the skins. Mash the ghee into the potatoes using a fork, then stir in the scallions, garlic, dill, parsley, nutritional yeast, chives, remaining 1 teaspoon salt, and the pepper. Add the broccoli and chicken and fold into the potato mixture.

Scoop the potato filling into the reserved potato skins and place them upright on the baking sheet. Bake for 20 minutes, or until the edges of the potatoes are lightly golden.

Whole30

Gluten-Free

Nut-Free

# Pizza Verde

Serves 2 to 4

1 (10-inch) store-bought pizza crust

¼ cup pizza sauce

4 ounces fresh burrata cheese

½ cup pitted Castelvetrano olives, halved

⅛ teaspoon red pepper flakes

5 fresh basil leaves, chopped

1 teaspoon extra-virgin olive oil, for drizzling

½ teaspoon flaky sea salt (I like Maldon)

This is my husband's and my go-to on pizza night at the Smith house. Yes, we still have pizza night. On a regular basis. While it isn't a part of my *everyday* diet, it is part of my Food Freedom. It's not just a meal, but a time for us to hang out with the kids in the kitchen and make our own custom pies (ours are delicious, while the kids' end up . . . odd at best). I opt for a store-bought pizza crust these days. There are so many ready-made options available, from cauliflower crusts to Paleo to gluten-free, that it's a dream come true for a slightly lazy person like myself. Just choose what best fits your needs!

Preheat the oven according to the pizza crust manufacturer's instructions.

Spread the pizza sauce over the crust and scatter with the burrata. Top the pizza with the olive halves and red pepper flakes and bake according to the pizza crust manufacturer's instructions, typically 10 to 12 minutes.

Sprinkle the pizza with the basil, drizzle with the olive oil, and season with the salt. Slice into wedges and serve.

Vegetarian
Nut-Free

# Zucchini "Street" Tacos with Poblano Crema

Serves 8

**For the roasted sweet potatoes:**

2 medium sweet potatoes, peeled and cut into bite-size cubes

1 tablespoon extra-virgin olive oil

1 teaspoon salt

½ teaspoon smoked paprika

¼ teaspoon ground chipotle

**For the slaw:**

¼ cup 1-Minute Mayonnaise (page 195)

2 teaspoons fresh lime juice

1 teaspoon honey

¼ teaspoon salt

3 cups store-bought cabbage slaw mix or shredded cabbage

**For the poblano crema:**

½ fresh poblano pepper

½ cup 1-Minute Mayonnaise (page 195)

½ cup coarsely chopped fresh cilantro

1 garlic clove, chopped

1 teaspoon unsweetened almond milk

1 teaspoon fresh lime juice

½ teaspoon salt

**For the grilled corn:**

1½ teaspoons extra-virgin olive oil

3 ears corn

2 teaspoons salt

Vegetarian

Gluten-Free

Dairy-Free

These tacos are just as delicious and indulgent as ones you might find at an authentic street taco truck. The substance of the charred veggies combined with the brightness of some zesty slaw make an awesome pair. There's nothing I love more than a good taco, but when you can make a taco that is satisfying *and* doesn't make you feel heavy and gross after, I'm so game.

**For the roasted sweet potatoes:** Preheat the oven to 425°F. Line a large baking sheet with parchment paper.

In a large bowl, combine the sweet potatoes, olive oil, salt, paprika, and chipotle and toss to coat. Spread the sweet potatoes in an even layer over the prepared baking sheet. Bake for 25 to 30 minutes, until the sweet potatoes are tender and lightly browned. Set aside.

**For the slaw:** In a large bowl, whisk together the mayonnaise, lime juice, honey, and salt. Add the slaw to the dressing, toss to coat, and set aside.

**For the poblano crema:** Preheat a grill or grill pan over medium heat.

Using a pair of tongs, place the poblano over an open flame (such as a grill or gas stovetop burner). Turn the poblano every 5 to 7 minutes, until each side is charred. Keeping the grill on, remove the poblano from the heat and wrap it in a wet paper towel. Allow the pepper to rest for 4 to 5 minutes, then use the paper towel to gently rub off the charred skin.

Coarsely chop the charred poblano and put it in a medium bowl. Add the mayonnaise, cilantro, garlic, almond milk, lime juice, and salt. Using an immersion blender, blend until smooth. Set the crema aside.

**For the grilled corn:** Brush the olive oil onto the corn and sprinkle with the salt.

Place the corn onto the grill grate or in a grill pan and cook for 15 to 20 minutes, turning every 5 minutes. Remove the corn from the heat and cut the kernels from the cob. Transfer the kernels to a bowl and set aside.

**For the grilled zucchini:** In a large bowl, combine the melted butter, chili powder, salt, and paprika. Add the zucchini and toss to coat. Place the seasoned zucchini on the hot grill or grill pan and cook for 3 to 4 minutes on each side. Remove from the heat and cut each piece in half crosswise.

**For the grilled zucchini:**

4 tablespoons unsalted butter or ghee, melted

1 tablespoon chili powder

1 tablespoon salt

1½ teaspoons smoked paprika

3 medium zucchini, quartered lengthwise

**To assemble:**

8 corn tortillas

½ cup coarsely chopped fresh cilantro

½ cup crumbled cotija cheese

**To assemble:** Place the corn tortillas on the grill or in the grill pan and heat for 30 seconds per side. Remove from the heat.

Evenly distribute the slaw among the tortillas and top with the sweet potatoes, corn, and zucchini. Drizzle the poblano crema over each taco and top with the cilantro and cotija cheese.

GREAT FOR LEFTOVERS! ★★★

# Chinese Takeout Spaghetti Squash

Serves 2 to 4

2½ teaspoons extra-virgin olive oil

½ medium spaghetti squash, halved and seeded (see Note, page 155)

2½ teaspoons salt

½ teaspoon freshly ground black pepper

1¼ pounds ground pork

¼ teaspoon garlic powder

3 cups shredded green cabbage (about ¼ head)

½ cup shredded carrots (about 2 medium)

3 scallions, sliced

1 (3-inch) piece fresh ginger, peeled and finely grated

2 tablespoons coconut aminos, plus more for serving

2 teaspoons toasted sesame oil

1 teaspoon fish sauce

2 garlic cloves, minced

1 teaspoon sesame seeds, toasted (see Tip), for serving

Back in the day, Chinese takeout was my jam. Who doesn't crave all the salty, greasy treasures hiding in those white takeout boxes? While I still get those cravings, I realize now that I can replicate a lot of the same flavors at home with cleaner ingredients. A great thing about Chinese cuisine is that there are usually lots of vegetables in each dish. All that's left for you to do is remove the stuff that makes you feel less than stellar, and you're golden!

Take note: Not all coconut aminos are created equal. Some have a sweeter, smokier flavor and some are a bit saltier than others. Feel free to add more at the end for an additional hit of flavor, if desired.

Preheat the oven to 425°F. Line a small baking sheet with parchment paper.

Drizzle 1½ teaspoons of the olive oil over the squash and sprinkle with ¼ teaspoon of the salt and the pepper. Arrange the squash on the prepared baking sheet and bake for 35 minutes, until it is fork-tender and the edges are slightly browned. Let cool. When the spaghetti squash is cool enough to handle, use a fork to gently scrape the flesh out into strands. Transfer to a large bowl and set aside.

In a large skillet over medium-high heat, heat the remaining 1 teaspoon oil. Add the pork, 1¼ teaspoons of the salt, and the garlic powder and cook, gently breaking up the meat with a wooden spoon, for about 2 minutes. Reduce the heat to medium and cook, stirring continuously, for 5 to 7 minutes more, until the pork is cooked through. Use a slotted spoon to transfer the pork to a bowl and set aside. Drain any liquid from the pan, if necessary.

Add the cabbage, carrots, scallions, ginger, coconut aminos, sesame oil, fish sauce, and remaining 1 teaspoon salt to the same skillet and cook, stirring frequently, until the vegetables are softened, 5 to 6 minutes. Add the minced garlic and cook, stirring, for 1 minute more.

Add the pork and vegetables and toss to combine.

Paleo

Whole30

Gluten-Free

Dairy-Free

Nut-Free

Garnish with the toasted sesame seeds and additional coconut aminos, if desired, and serve.

> **Tip** To toast sesame seeds, heat a small skillet over medium-low heat and spread the sesame seeds into an even layer in the pan. Cook, stirring the sesame seeds continuously, until they are slightly golden and toasted, 3 to 4 minutes. Transfer to a plate and let cool.

GREAT FOR
LEFTOVERS!
★ ★ ★

# Pork Loin with Caramelized Onions + Applesauce

## Serves 4 to 6

4 garlic cloves, minced

1 teaspoon chopped fresh rosemary

1 teaspoon chopped fresh thyme

½ teaspoon freshly ground black pepper

2 pounds boneless pork loin

3 teaspoons salt

2 teaspoons extra-virgin olive oil

1 medium yellow onion, sliced (about 1 cup)

3 Granny Smith apples, peeled, cored, and diced

1 teaspoon apple cider vinegar

1 vanilla bean pod, split lengthwise and seeds scraped, or 1 teaspoon pure vanilla extract (see Note)

While my recipes are kinda like my kids—I can't pick a favorite—I might have to make an exception for this one. This is one of those Whole30 recipes that seems too good to be true. I absolutely adore the light sweetness of the apples and caramelized onions on top of a fat, juicy piece of pork. Complete with the pork's salty, lightly herbed crust, it's pretty much heaven on a plate.

Preheat the oven to 400°F. Line a baking dish with aluminum foil.

In a small bowl, combine the garlic, rosemary, thyme, and pepper to create a paste.

Season the pork with 2 teaspoons of the salt. Use a knife to cut several small openings into the pork flesh and stuff each with ½ teaspoon of the garlic paste. Pat the remaining garlic paste onto the surface of the pork. Place the pork, fat-side down, in the prepared baking dish and roast for 30 minutes. Flip the pork, then roast for 20 minutes more, or until the internal temperature reaches 145°F.

While the pork is roasting, in a large skillet over medium heat, heat the olive oil. Add the onion and remaining 1 teaspoon salt and cook, stirring frequently, until the onion is soft and caramelized, 12 to 15 minutes.

In a large saucepan over medium heat, stir together the apples, vinegar, vanilla bean seeds, and ½ cup water. Cook, stirring frequently, until the apples break down into a chunky sauce, 5 to 7 minutes.

Once the pork loin has finished roasting, let it rest, covered, for 10 minutes.

Cut the pork into 2-inch-thick slices and serve topped with the apple sauce and caramelized onion.

 **Note** *If you're doing a Whole30, make sure to use the vanilla bean instead of the extract.*

Paleo

Whole30

Gluten-Free

Dairy-Free

Nut-Free

# Strawberry + Balsamic Salmon

Serves 2 to 4

2 teaspoons extra-virgin olive oil, plus more for grill

2 pounds skin-on salmon fillets

1 teaspoon salt

½ cup balsamic vinegar

2 cups fresh strawberries, hulled and sliced

6 fresh basil leaves, chopped

If someone would have told me back in the day that I'd be eating fish and fruit together on the same plate, let alone in the same bite, I would have thought they were nuts. But I would have been oh-so-wrong, because it's an unexpectedly beautiful pairing.

Heat a grill to medium-high or heat a large grill pan over medium-high heat. Lightly brush the grill or pan with olive oil.

Brush the salmon fillets with 2 teaspoons of olive oil and season with the salt. Place the fillets skin-side down on the grill and cook, covered, until cooked through but not dry, 6 minutes. Flip the salmon and cook for 3 to 5 minutes more, depending on thickness.

In a small saucepan over medium heat, heat the vinegar until slightly syrupy, 10 to 12 minutes.

Top the grilled salmon with the strawberries, basil, and a drizzle of the balsamic reduction and serve.

Paleo
Whole30
Gluten-Free
Dairy-Free
Nut-Free

# Roasted Red Pepper Zoodles + Beef

Serves 4 to 6

2½ teaspoons extra-virgin olive oil

1 pound 80% lean ground beef

3½ teaspoons salt

1 cup diced yellow onion (about 1 medium)

3 garlic cloves, minced

1 cup raw cashew pieces, soaked in hot water for 1 hour and drained

½ cup unsweetened almond milk

1 teaspoon fresh lemon juice

¼ teaspoon freshly ground black pepper

¾ cup jarred roasted red peppers (about 3 large), drained

4 medium zucchini, spiralized using a medium blade

¼ teaspoon red pepper flakes, plus more for serving

¼ cup chopped fresh basil, for serving

The first time I made zucchini noodles, I steamed them. In the words of Julia Roberts in *Pretty Woman*: "Big mistake. Big. *Huge.*" Steaming the noodles rendered them soggy and left me wondering what all the zoodle hype was about. Soon after, I learned that the best way to cook zoodles is not to steam them, but to add them directly to the heated sauce you're using. They're left slightly tender and cooked, but still retain the perfect amount of bite to stand up to any sauce.

In a large Dutch oven over medium-high heat, heat 2 teaspoons of the olive oil. Add the ground beef and 1 teaspoon of the salt. Cook, gently breaking up the meat with a wooden spoon, until browned and cooked through, 7 to 9 minutes. Use a slotted spoon to transfer the ground beef to a bowl and set aside.

Use a paper towel to wipe out the Dutch oven and return it to medium heat. Add the remaining ½ teaspoon oil. Add the onion and cook, stirring, until softened and lightly browned at the edges, 6 to 7 minutes. Add the garlic and cook, stirring, until tender and fragrant, 1 minute. Use a slotted spoon to transfer the onion and garlic to a blender and add the cashews, almond milk, lemon juice, black pepper, and 1 teaspoon of the salt. Blend on high for about 1 minute, until the sauce is creamy. Add the roasted red peppers and pulse until they are well combined.

Transfer the sauce to the Dutch oven over medium-low heat. Stir in the ground beef and cook until the sauce is heated through, 5 minutes. Add the spiralized zucchini, the remaining 1 teaspoon salt, and the red pepper flakes and toss to coat. Cook the zucchini noodles until tender but not mushy, 2 to 3 minutes.

To serve, top with the basil and additional red pepper flakes, if desired.

Paleo

Whole30

Dairy-Free

# Lemon + Herb Roasted Chicken Thighs

## Serves 4 to 6

8 bone-in, skin-on chicken thighs (about 3 pounds)

1 tablespoon extra-virgin olive oil

1 tablespoon salt

1 tablespoon chopped fresh thyme, plus more for serving

1½ teaspoons lemon pepper

2 teaspoons fresh lemon juice

4 garlic cloves, minced

2 lemons, sliced

Roasted chicken thighs are simply the best. They're brimming with flavor and hard to overcook, so even the greenest of chefs can master a perfectly roasted chicken thigh. Add some lemon and herbs, and you're as good as gold. If you're looking for a side to pair this with, I recommend the Roasted Broccolini with Lemon + Olives (page 148).

Preheat the oven to 425°F. Line a baking sheet with parchment paper.

In a large bowl, combine the chicken thighs, olive oil, salt, thyme, lemon pepper, garlic, and lemon juice and toss to coat well.

Place the lemon slices in an even layer on the prepared baking sheet. Place the chicken thighs over the lemon slices and bake for 40 minutes.

Move the baking sheet to the top rack, set the oven to broil, and broil the chicken thighs for 30 seconds to 1 minute to crisp the chicken skin, being careful not to burn it.

Garnish with additional thyme, if desired.

Paleo

Whole30

Gluten-Free

Dairy-Free

Nut-Free

# Instant Pot Asian Braised Short Ribs

### Serves 4

2 pounds bone-in short ribs

4 teaspoons salt

1 tablespoon extra-virgin olive oil

1 cup chopped sweet onion
(about 1 medium)

1 cup coconut aminos

1 tablespoon toasted sesame oil

1 tablespoon rice wine vinegar

1 tablespoon fish sauce

1 tablespoon honey

2 garlic cloves, minced

1 scallion, thinly sliced, for garnish

1 teaspoon sesame seeds, toasted
(see Tip, page 111), for garnish

For the longest time, I was apprehensive about making short ribs. I always ordered them at restaurants but felt they weren't something I would be able to easily cook at home.

Until I discovered the Instant Pot.

I soon realized the magic of pressure cooking and decided it was time to try my hand at some short ribs. And they tasted just like the ones that I ordered at restaurants for so many years.

In this version, I add some Asian-inspired flavors to take things to the next level. If you can add ingredients to a pot and press a couple of buttons, you're ensured a batch of short ribs that taste like they came from your favorite restaurant.

Season the short ribs with 2 teaspoons of the salt.

In a cast-iron skillet over medium-high heat, heat the olive oil. Place the short ribs in the skillet and sear each side for about 10 seconds. Transfer the short ribs to the Instant Pot. Add the onion, coconut aminos, sesame oil, vinegar, fish sauce, honey, garlic, and remaining 2 teaspoons salt. Select the "Meat/Stew" setting on the Instant Pot and cook on high pressure for 1 hour. Let the pressure release naturally.

Use tongs to remove the ribs from the Instant Pot and transfer them to a serving platter. Select the "Sauté" setting and reduce the cooking liquid for 10 minutes.

To serve, pour the reduced cooking liquid over the short ribs and garnish with the scallion and toasted sesame seeds.

**Note** *To modify for Whole30, omit the honey.*

Paleo

Whole30-
Compliant If
Modified

Dairy-Free

Nut-Free

# Butternut Squash Enchiladas

**Serves 4 to 6**

4 cups cubed peeled butternut squash

½ medium yellow onion, chopped (about ½ cup)

1 tablespoon extra-virgin olive oil, plus more for greasing

1½ teaspoons salt

½ teaspoon ground chipotle

1 cup green enchilada sauce

1 medium Hass avocado

1 cup fresh cilantro leaves, coarsely chopped, plus more for serving

1 (4-ounce) can mild green chiles

2 garlic cloves

2 tablespoons unsweetened almond milk

1 tablespoon fresh lime juice (from about ½ lime)

6 (6-inch) corn, flour, or Paleo tortillas

¼ cup crumbled goat cheese, plus more for serving

My dear friend Annie and I take an annual trip to LA each October. We pretend we're cool 25-year-olds again and try the bougiest restaurants and any other ridiculously trendy LA-type activities we can find. Last year, our travels landed us at Gracias Madre, a vegan Mexican restaurant in West Hollywood. Vegan?! What's a Paleo food blogger doing in a vegan restaurant? I know, I know—but there were lots of perfectly prepared veggies and amazing flavor combinations. When Annie ordered butternut squash enchiladas that blew both of us away, I knew I had to re-create them back at home. So here they are. Annie, this one's for you!

Preheat the oven to 400°F. Line two large baking sheets with parchment paper.

In a large bowl, toss the butternut squash, onion, olive oil, 1 teaspoon of the salt, and the chipotle. Spread the squash and onion in an even layer over the prepared baking sheets and roast for 35 minutes, or until the vegetables are tender and the edges are golden. Let the vegetables cool and reduce the oven temperature to 375°F.

In a blender or food processor, combine the enchilada sauce, avocado, half the cilantro, half the green chiles, the garlic, almond milk, lime juice, and remaining ½ teaspoon salt and blend on high for 20 seconds, or until the sauce is smooth and creamy. Set aside.

Transfer the roasted butternut squash and onion to a large bowl and combine with the remaining cilantro and green chiles. Stir.

Lightly grease an 8 by 10-inch baking dish with olive oil.

Spread ¼ cup of the roasted vegetable filling down the center of a tortilla. Sprinkle the filling with a pinch of goat cheese and roll up the tortilla. Place the rolled tortilla seam-side down in the prepared baking dish and repeat with the remaining tortillas. Pour the enchilada sauce over top of the rolled tortillas, making sure to cover the entire dish, and bake for 20 minutes, or until the sauce begins to bubble.

To serve, top with additional cilantro or goat cheese.

Paleo
Gluten-Free
Vegan
Vegetarian

**GREAT FOR LEFTOVERS!**

# Brussels Sprout Stir-Fry

Who doesn't love a good stir-fry? Throw in some veggies, some meat, and lots of flavor, and you have yourself a meal!

### Serves 4

8 cups Brussels sprouts (about 1¼ pounds), sliced into thirds

3 tablespoons extra-virgin olive oil

2¾ teaspoons salt

½ teaspoon freshly ground black pepper

1½ medium yellow onion, chopped (about ½ cup)

1 red bell pepper, sliced

1¼ pounds steak (flap or skirt steak), thinly sliced across the grain

**For the stir-fry sauce:**

½ cup coconut aminos

3 tablespoons apple cider vinegar

1 tablespoon coconut sugar (see Note)

1 teaspoon fish sauce

1 teaspoon toasted sesame oil

1 (2-inch) piece fresh ginger, peeled and finely grated

1 tablespoon arrowroot powder

Preheat the oven to 425°F. Line two large baking sheets with parchment paper.

Put the Brussels sprouts in a large bowl and toss with 2 tablespoons of the olive oil, 2 teaspoons of the salt, and the pepper. Spread the Brussels sprouts in an even layer over the prepared baking sheets. Roast for 20 to 22 minutes, until the Brussels sprouts are cooked through and some of the edges have browned.

In a large skillet over medium heat, heat 2 teaspoons of the olive oil. Add the onion and cook, stirring, until tender, 4 to 5 minutes. Add the bell pepper to the pan and cook, stirring frequently, for 4 minutes more.

Season the beef with the remaining 1¼ teaspoons salt.

Push the onion and pepper to one side of the pan. Add the remaining 1 teaspoon oil and the seasoned beef strips and cook, stirring frequently, until the meat has cooked through, 5 to 6 minutes. Once cooked through, drain the excess liquid from the pan and add the roasted Brussels sprouts.

**For the stir-fry sauce:** In a saucepan over medium heat, combine the coconut aminos, vinegar, coconut sugar, fish sauce, sesame oil, ginger, and 2 tablespoons water. Whisk until the coconut sugar has dissolved and the sauce is hot, 2 to 4 minutes. While whisking, gradually sprinkle the arrowroot powder into the sauce and whisk until thickened, 2 to 3 minutes.

Pour the sauce over the stir-fry and stir to coat well. Serve.

 **Note** To modify for Whole30, omit the coconut sugar from the stir-fry sauce.

 **Tip** If there are any lumps from the arrowroot powder in the stir-fry sauce, pour the sauce through a fine-mesh strainer prior to adding it to the stir-fry.

Paleo

Whole30-Compliant If Modified

Gluten-Free

Dairy-Free

Nut-Free

# Mustard-Roasted Chicken Drums

## Serves 4 to 6

2 pounds bone-in, skin-on chicken drumsticks

⅔ cup ghee or salted butter, melted (see Note)

½ cup grated sweet onion (about ½ medium)

¼ cup Dijon mustard

2 teaspoons salt

1 teaspoon chopped fresh thyme

Tangy, salty, and otherwise flavorful recipes like this prove that you don't need to feel deprived when you're eating well or doing a Whole30. Nor do you have to plan your meals far ahead of time. Chances are, you've already got these ingredients stocked in your pantry. The marinade I use here works well with any cut of chicken, but also salmon, so don't hesitate to play around with it.

In a 1-gallon zip-top plastic bag or large bowl, combine the chicken, melted ghee, onion, mustard, salt, and thyme. Set aside to marinate at room temperature for 1 hour.

Preheat the oven to 425°F.

Arrange the marinated drumsticks on a broiler pan. Pour any remaining marinade over the chicken. (It's okay if the ghee solidified slightly during the marinating process.)

Bake for 35 minutes, or until the chicken reaches an internal temperature of 165°F. Let rest for 5 minutes prior to serving.

**Note** *If you're doing a Whole30, make sure to use ghee instead of butter.*

Paleo

Whole30

Gluten-Free

Nut-Free

# Chimichurri Taco Peppers

Serves 4 to 6

**For the ground beef:**

2 bacon slices, chopped

1 pound 85% lean ground beef

1½ tablespoons smoked paprika

1 tablespoon chili powder

2 teaspoons salt, plus more to taste

½ teaspoon ground cumin

¼ teaspoon freshly ground black pepper

½ cup chopped white onion (about ½ medium)

2 to 3 teaspoons extra-virgin olive oil

8 ounces cremini mushrooms, chopped

**For the chimichurri sauce:**

½ cup extra-virgin olive oil

⅓ cup chopped fresh cilantro, plus extra for garnish (optional)

¼ cup coarsely chopped fresh parsley

1 teaspoon lime zest (see Tip)

2 tablespoons fresh lime juice (about 2 limes)

½ teaspoon chili powder

½ teaspoon salt

⅛ teaspoon red pepper flakes

**To assemble:**

3 bell peppers (any color), halved lengthwise

Paleo
Whole30
Gluten-Free
Dairy-Free
Nut-Free

Did you know chimichurri is the new pesto? Because it is. Chimichurri is pesto's cooler, hipper cousin, and it's here to stay. This is the perfect prep-in-advance recipe. You can make the taco filling and the chimichurri sauce ahead of time and work through them throughout the week. Easy to make, easy to pack, and even easier to eat!

**For the ground beef:** In a large skillet or Dutch oven over medium-high heat, cook the bacon, stirring frequently, until the fat renders and the meat begins to brown, 3 to 4 minutes. Add the ground beef and cook, gently breaking it up with a wooden spoon or spatula as it cooks. Season the bacon and beef with the smoked paprika, chili powder, 1½ teaspoons of the salt, the cumin, and black pepper and stir to thoroughly combine. Cook, stirring occasionally, until it is cooked through, 6 to 7 minutes. Use a slotted spoon to transfer the meat to a paper towel–lined plate. Drain two-thirds of the fat from the pan.

Reduce the heat to medium and add the onion to the pan and cook, stirring, until tender and lightly browned, 6 to 7 minutes. If the pan looks dry, add 1 teaspoon of the olive oil. Remove from the heat.

In separate large skillet over medium heat, heat the remaining 2 teaspoons olive oil. Add the mushrooms and season with the remaining ½ teaspoon salt. Cook, stirring frequently, until the mushrooms are tender, 7 to 8 minutes.

Add the ground beef and cooked mushrooms to the skillet with the onion and toss to combine. Season with salt.

**For the chimichurri sauce:** In a medium bowl, combine the olive oil, cilantro, parsley, lime zest, lime juice, chili powder, salt, and red pepper flakes.

**To assemble:** Scoop the ground beef mixture into the bell pepper halves and generously drizzle with the chimichurri sauce. Sprinkle with chopped cilantro, if desired.

**Note** *For an additional layer of flavor, drizzle some Chipotle Crema (page 208) over the top.*

**Tip** *Always zest your citrus prior to juicing. It's easy to forget, so I'm often left trying to grate squishy citrus rinds. Don't be like me.*

# Red Curry Turkey Lettuce Cups

Serves 3 or 4

1½ heads cauliflower, cut into florets, or 6 cups store-bought cauliflower rice

5 teaspoons extra-virgin olive oil

2¾ teaspoons salt

1 medium yellow onion, chopped (about 1 cup)

1 yellow bell pepper, very thinly sliced

1¼ pounds 90% lean ground turkey

1 teaspoon garlic powder

1 teaspoon ground ginger

¼ teaspoon freshly ground black pepper

1 cup full-fat coconut milk

4 ounces red curry paste (I prefer Thai Kitchen, which is Whole30-compliant)

⅓ cup chopped fresh basil, plus more for garnish

6 iceberg lettuce leaves

Whether you're looking for a portable lunch to take to work or a quick dinner after soccer practice, these curry lettuce cups are a great make-ahead option for busy people. Simply make the cauliflower rice and turkey curry in advance and use it throughout the week to stuff into lettuce cups.

If using fresh cauliflower, in a food processor, pulse the cauliflower florets until rice-like in consistency. Set aside.

In a large skillet over medium heat, heat 2 teaspoons of the olive oil. Add the cauliflower rice, 1 teaspoon of the salt, and ¼ cup water and stir to combine. Cook the cauliflower, stirring frequently, until tender but not soggy, 7 to 9 minutes. Transfer the cauliflower rice to a bowl.

Add 2 teaspoons of the olive oil to the pan and heat over medium heat. Once the oil is hot, add the onion and ½ teaspoon of the salt and cook, stirring, until the onion starts to soften, 3 to 4 minutes. Add the bell pepper and stir to combine. Cook, stirring, until the onion is lightly browned and the bell pepper has softened, 3 to 4 minutes.

In a medium bowl, combine the ground turkey, garlic powder, ginger, black pepper, and remaining 1¼ teaspoons and use your clean hands to mix well.

Push the onion and bell pepper to the side of the pan and add the remaining 1 teaspoon oil. Once the oil is hot, add the ground turkey mixture and cook, breaking up the meat with a spatula, until the meat is cooked through, 5 to 6 minutes. Add the coconut milk, red curry paste, and basil and stir to combine.

To serve, divide the cauliflower evenly among the lettuce leaves and top each with the red curry turkey sauce. Top with additional basil, if desired.

Paleo
Whole30
Gluten-Free
Dairy-Free
Nut-Free

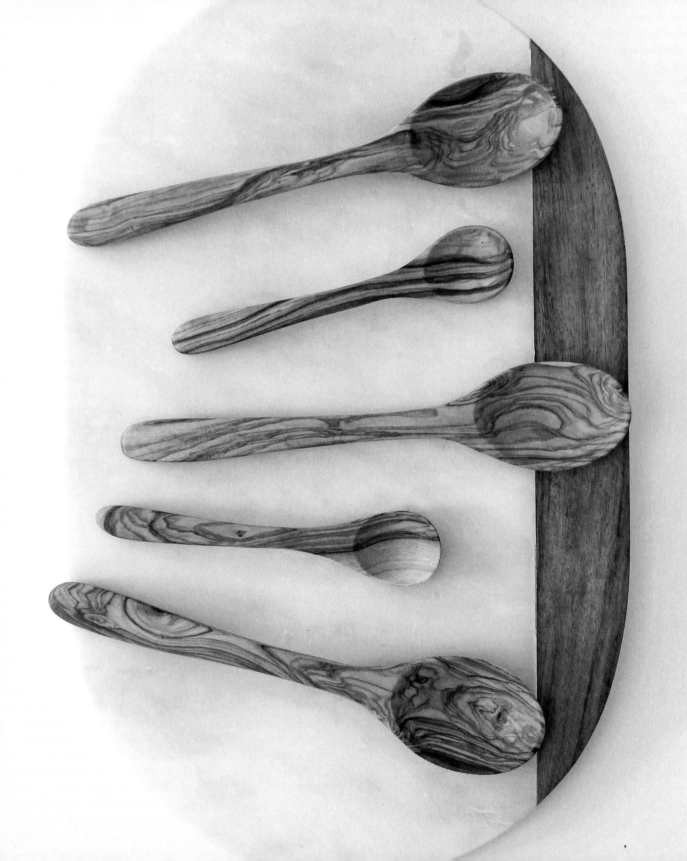

# Veggies + Sides

# Spanish Tortilla with Romesco Sauce

### Serves 4 to 6

**For the Spanish tortilla:**

1½ cups plus 2 tablespoons extra-virgin olive oil

2 pounds yellow potatoes, peeled and sliced into ⅛- to ¼-inch-thick discs

1 medium yellow onion, chopped (about 1 cup)

1 teaspoon salt

6 large eggs, beaten

**For the romesco sauce:**

1 red bell pepper

½ cup 1-Minute Mayonnaise (page 195)

3 garlic cloves

1¼ teaspoons salt

¼ cup chopped fresh parsley, for garnish

One of my favorite recipes my mom made for us growing up was her Spanish tortilla. My grandmother, who's from Madrid, taught her how to make it, and my mom did the same for me. While the technique may seem tricky, Spanish tortilla is, at its core, a simple dish we can all master. Even better, it's naturally Paleo and Whole30-compliant.

**For the Spanish tortilla:** In a large Dutch oven or stockpot over medium heat, heat 1½ cups of the olive oil. Add the potatoes, onion, and salt and stir to coat with the oil. Cook, stirring occasionally, until the potatoes are tender and golden brown, 20 to 25 minutes. Remove from the heat and transfer to a large bowl.

In a 10-inch nonstick skillet over medium-low heat, heat the remaining 2 tablespoons oil. Add the cooked potatoes and onion to the pan and pour the eggs over the top. Using a spatula, gently stir the mixture to fully incorporate the eggs and vegetables. Cook, stirring occasionally, until the eggs start to set, 2 to 3 minutes. Cook, without stirring, until the edges have begun to set and most of the tortilla has cooked through, 9 to 11 minutes.

Using a spatula, gently loosen the sides of the tortilla from the pan. Place a large plate facedown over the pan. Turn the pan and plate over together to cleanly flip the tortilla onto the plate. Carefully slide the tortilla back into the pan, uncooked-side down, and cook for 4 to 5 minutes more. Slide the tortilla onto the plate and let cool for 10 minutes.

**For the romesco sauce:** Hold the red pepper directly over the flame of a gas stovetop or set it under the broiler until each side is charred, about 2 minutes per side. Wrap the charred red pepper in a wet paper towel and let it sit for 15 minutes. Remove and discard the charred skin, stem, and seeds. Transfer the flesh to a blender or a food processor. Add the mayonnaise, garlic, and salt and blend on high for 10 to 20 seconds, until the sauce is well combined. (Alternatively, combine the ingredients in a medium bowl and blend using an immersion blender or handheld mixer.)

To serve, slice the tortilla into wedges, top with some of the roasted red pepper sauce, and sprinkle with the parsley.

Whole30

Gluten-Free

Vegetarian

Dairy-Free

Nut-Free

# Cauliflower Rice Tabbouleh

### Serves 4 to 6

1½ heads cauliflower, cut into florets
or 6 cups pre-riced cauliflower

1 tablespoon plus 2 teaspoons
extra-virgin olive oil

2 teaspoons salt

2 cups shredded cooked chicken
(light and dark meat)

1 cup pitted kalamata olives, halved

1 cup cherry tomatoes, halved

1 red bell pepper, diced

⅓ cup chopped red onion
(about ⅓ medium)

3 tablespoons finely chopped
fresh parsley

2 tablespoons finely chopped
fresh mint

2 teaspoons grated lemon zest

1 teaspoon fresh lemon juice

Cauliflower has become the workhorse of all vegetables. You can flatten it into a pizza crust, grate it into rice, or mash it in lieu of potatoes. Here I use it to replace bulgur wheat. Its neutral flavor makes it the perfect companion to a zillion (yes, I counted) different dish variations.

In a food processor, pulse the cauliflower florets until broken down to a rice-like consistency.

In a large sauté pan or skillet over medium heat, heat 1 tablespoon of the olive oil. Add the cauliflower rice, ⅓ cup water, and 1 teaspoon of the salt. Stir to combine and cook, stirring occasionally, until tender but not soggy, 5 to 6 minutes.

Transfer the cauliflower rice to a large bowl and toss for 2 to 3 minutes to release the steam and any additional moisture. Refrigerate for 1 to 2 hours, until completely cool.

Add the remaining 1 teaspoon salt, the chicken, olives, tomatoes, bell pepper, onion, parsley, mint, lemon zest, and lemon juice to the bowl with the cauliflower rice and stir to combine.

Drizzle with the remaining 2 teaspoons olive oil and serve.

Paleo
Whole30
Gluten-Free
Dairy-Free
Nut-Free

# Spicy Charred Green Beans

Serves 4

⅓ cup crushed almond pieces

1 tablespoon garlic chili paste

1 tablespoon coconut aminos

1 teaspoon toasted sesame oil

1 teaspoon honey

½ teaspoon salt

1 pound green beans, ends trimmed

2 teaspoons extra-virgin olive oil

There's not much I won't try to grill up. Some are fails, but these green beans are a definite win, so much so that you may never want to go back to steaming them again.

In a large bowl, stir together the almond pieces, garlic chili paste, coconut aminos, sesame oil, honey, and salt. Set aside.

In a separate large bowl, toss the green beans with the olive oil to coat.

Heat a grill to medium-high or heat a grill pan over medium-high heat.

Place the green beans on the grill or pan in an even layer and cook until the green beans are lightly charred and tender, 8 to 10 minutes.

Transfer the cooked green beans to the bowl with the almond sauce and toss to coat. Serve.

Paleo

Gluten-Free

Vegan

Vegetarian

Dairy-Free

# Apple Cider Vinegar–Braised Collards with Mushrooms + Shallots

Serves 4

4 teaspoons extra-virgin olive oil

1 large shallot, sliced

10 ounces sliced cremini mushrooms

1½ teaspoons salt

1 bunch collard greens, ribs removed and chopped (about 4 cups)

1 tablespoon apple cider vinegar

Braised greens make a perfect and nutrient-dense side dish for so many proteins, and they're quite easy to whip up. I prefer mine to have a little bit of bite to them, so I cook them for closer to 15 minutes. If you like yours to be softer, cook them closer to 20 minutes.

In a large skillet over medium heat, heat 1 teaspoon of the olive oil. Add the shallot and cook, stirring frequently, until tender and slightly caramelized, 4 to 5 minutes.

While the shallot is cooking, in a medium skillet over medium heat, heat the remaining 3 teaspoons oil. Add the mushrooms and 1 teaspoon of the salt and cook, stirring frequently, until tender and cooked through, 4 to 5 minutes.

Transfer the cooked mushrooms to the pan with the shallot. Add the collard greens, vinegar, and remaining ½ teaspoon salt. Stir. Reduce the heat to medium-low, cover, and cook, stirring occasionally, until tender, 15 to 20 minutes. Serve alongside your favorite protein.

Paleo
Whole30
Gluten-Free
Vegan
Vegetarian
Dairy-Free
Nut-Free

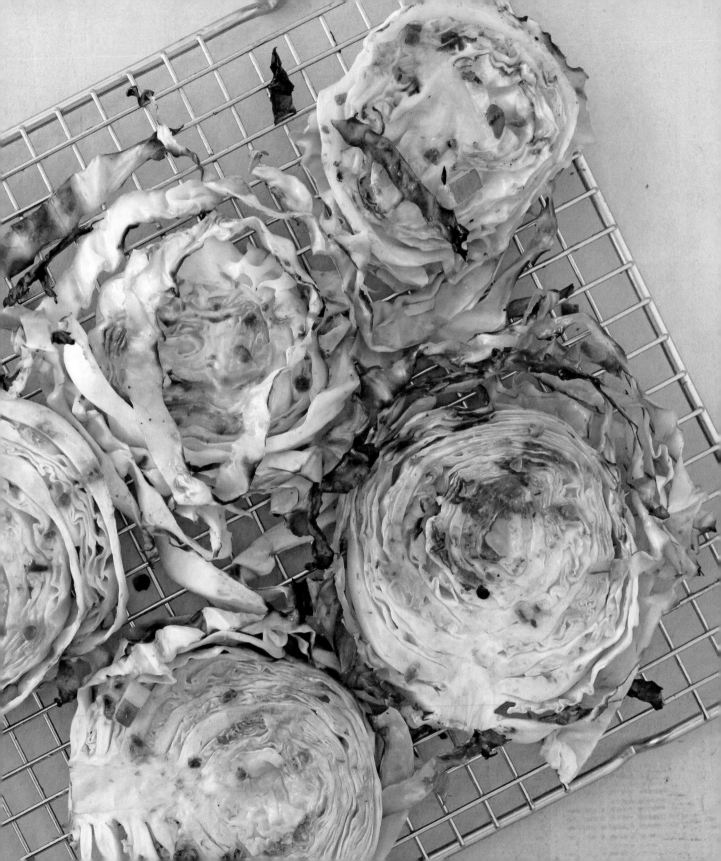

# Grilled Cabbage Steaks

Serves 4

⅓ cup extra-virgin olive oil

⅓ cup finely chopped red onion
(about ⅓ medium)

2 tablespoons Dijon mustard

2 tablespoons capers, drained,
rinsed, and chopped

2 teaspoons white wine vinegar

1 teaspoon salt

1 head green cabbage, sliced
vertically into ½-inch-wide steaks

For so long, we shredded our cabbage and ignored all the different ways we could cook it up, like sliced and grilled! The crispy edges of these "steaks" paired with a zesty mustard sauce make it the perfect side dish for any summer barbecue.

Heat a grill to medium or heat a grill pan over medium heat.

In a medium bowl, combine the olive oil, onion, mustard, capers, vinegar, and salt.

Brush the sauce over one side of each cabbage steak and place the cabbage steaks sauce-side down on the grill or grill pan. Brush the other side of the cabbage steaks with the sauce and cook for 10 to 15 minutes. Flip the cabbage and cook until the cabbage is tender and the edges are slightly charred, 10 to 15 minutes.

Serve with any remaining sauce brushed over the cabbage.

Paleo

Whole30

Gluten-Free

Vegan

Vegetarian

Dairy-Free

Nut-Free

# Roasted Delicata Squash with Herbs + Garlic

Serves 4

2 tablespoons plus 1 teaspoon ghee or salted butter, melted

6 garlic cloves, minced

2 teaspoons salt

1½ teaspoons fresh rosemary

1½ teaspoons fresh thyme

½ teaspoon freshly ground black pepper

2 pounds delicata squash, seeded and sliced into ¼-inch-thick discs

½ cup walnut pieces

One of my favorite fall veggies is delicata squash. I love roasting it up in a variety of ways, but my favorite is with a simple combination of herbs and garlic. If you can't find delicata squash at your local supermarket, never fear! These flavors work just as well with sweet potato discs. Simply slice your sweet potatoes into discs and increase the cooking time to 35 to 40 minutes, making sure to flip them halfway through.

Preheat the oven to 425°F. Line two baking sheets with parchment paper.

In a large bowl, combine 2 tablespoons of the melted ghee, the garlic, salt, rosemary, thyme, and pepper and stir to combine. Add the delicata squash and toss to coat the slices well.

In a separate bowl, combine the walnut pieces and remaining 1 teaspoon melted ghee and stir to coat the walnut pieces.

Place the delicata slices in a single layer on the prepared baking sheets and roast for 20 minutes. Flip the slices and add the coated walnuts to the pan over the squash. Roast for an additional 10 to 15 minutes until the squash is golden brown on the edges.

Paleo
Whole30
Gluten-Free
Dairy-Free
Vegetarian

# 3-Minute Cucumbers + Avocado

## Serves 4

1 tablespoon plus 1 teaspoon rice vinegar

2 teaspoons toasted sesame oil

2 teaspoons salt

1 medium cucumber, sliced

2 Hass avocados, sliced

1 cup mung bean sprouts

1 teaspoon sesame seeds, toasted (see Tip, page 111)

Sometimes you need a veggie side dish that you can whip up in no time. Granted, you can reach for a handful of baby carrots, but does that ever sound delicious?

This breezy little ditty may be easy to make, but it's loaded with flavor. Whip it up for lunches or dinners and serve it alongside your favorite protein.

And even better? No oven necessary!

Whisk together the vinegar, sesame oil, and salt in a bowl.

For each serving, put one-quarter of the cucumber slices, one-quarter of the avocado, and one-quarter of the mung bean sprouts on a plate. Drizzle with one-quarter of the dressing and top with a pinch of the toasted sesame seeds.

Paleo
Whole30
Gluten-Free
Dairy-Free
Nut-Free
Vegan
Vegetarian

# Chipotle-Lime Butternut Squash

## Serves 2 to 4

2 pounds pre-cut butternut squash crinkles (see Note)

½ cup chopped fresh cilantro, plus extra for garnish

Grated zest and juice of 2 limes, plus extra for serving

2 tablespoons extra-virgin olive oil

2 teaspoons ground chipotle

1 teaspoon salt

Butternut squash has gotten a bad rap as a boring ol' autumn vegetable, best used pureed into a soup. For the most part, butternut squash hasn't done much other than get souped or Thanksgiving-side-dished for years. But no more! I decided to give this funky-shaped squash a makeover and introduce it to some Mexican-inspired flavors we don't naturally pair it with, like chipotle chile and cilantro. I'd say it's a success, and I think you'll agree.

Preheat the oven to 425°F. Line two baking sheets with parchment paper.

In a large bowl, combine the butternut squash, cilantro, lime zest, lime juice, olive oil, chipotle, and salt and toss to coat. Spread the squash in an even layer over the prepared baking sheets. Roast for 25 to 30 minutes, until the squash is fork-tender and lightly browned. Serve garnished with cilantro and lime wedges for squeezing.

**Note** *If you're unable to find pre-cut butternut squash crinkles at your local grocery store, don't fret! You can still make this recipe using a whole butternut squash. Simply cut off the ends of the squash and peel it using a vegetable peeler. From there, cut the squash down the center lengthwise and scoop the seeds out. Cut the squash into 2-inch spears and proceed with the the recipe.*

Paleo

Whole30

Vegetarian

Vegan

Dairy-Free

Nut-Free

# Curried Cauliflower

**Serves 4**

1 head cauliflower, cut into 1-inch florets

2 tablespoons extra-virgin olive oil

1½ teaspoons curry powder

½ teaspoon ground coriander

½ teaspoon ground cardamom

½ teaspoon salt

¼ cup golden raisins

2 tablespoons sliced almonds

1 tablespoon chopped fresh cilantro

Cauliflower is one of my favorite veggies to roast. Not only does it get perfectly browned bits of crispiness along its edges, but there are endless flavor combinations you can add to cauliflower—it's hard to get bored of it. While this recipe bursts with flavor from the curry powder, it's not spicy, so don't be afraid of introducing something adventurous like this to the kiddos!

Preheat the oven to 425°F. Line a large baking sheet with parchment paper.

In a large bowl, combine the cauliflower, olive oil, curry, coriander, cardamom, and salt and toss to evenly coat.

Spread the cauliflower into an even layer over the prepared baking sheet and roast for 20 minutes. Sprinkle the raisins and almonds over the cauliflower and roast for 5 minutes more, or until the cauliflower is tender and the edges have browned.

Transfer to a serving dish, sprinkle with the cilantro, and serve.

Paleo
Whole30
Gluten-Free
Vegan
Vegetarian
Dairy-Free

# Roasted Broccolini with Lemon + Olives

## Serves 4

1 pound broccolini

2 tablespoons extra-virgin olive oil

1 tablespoon fresh lemon juice

1 teaspoon lemon pepper

1 teaspoon salt

½ cup pitted kalamata olives

Lemon wedges, for serving

Quite honestly, I've never met a vegetable that doesn't taste better roasted rather than steamed. (Can you tell yet I'm not a fan of steaming them?) Broccolini is no exception. If you can't find broccolini at your local supermarket, you can easily substitute regular broccoli in its place.

Preheat the oven to 425°F. Line a baking sheet with parchment paper.

In a large bowl, combine the broccolini, olive oil, lemon juice, lemon pepper, and salt and toss to coat well. Place the broccolini in a single layer on the prepared baking sheet and roast for 15 minutes. Add the olives to the baking sheet and roast for 5 to 7 minutes more; the broccolini will be tender with lightly browned edges.

Serve with lemon wedges for squeezing over top.

Paleo

Whole30

Gluten-Free

Dairy-Free

Nut-Free

Vegan

Vegetarian

# Roasted Root Veggies

They're roast-y, they're homey, and they're healthy. What's not to love?

Preheat the oven to 425°F. Line two large baking sheets with parchment paper.

In a large bowl, combine the carrots, parsnips, beets, spring onions, olive oil, salt, rosemary, and thyme and toss to coat the vegetables with the oil and seasonings.

Spread the vegetables in an even layer over the prepared baking sheets and roast for 35 to 40 minutes, until tender and lightly browned on the edges.

To serve, transfer to a serving dish and top with the toasted pine nuts.

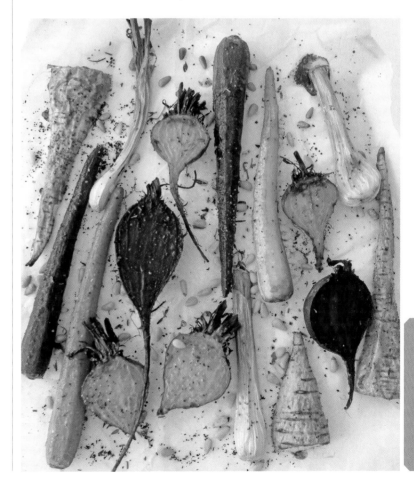

Paleo

Whole30

Gluten-Free

Vegan

Vegetarian

Dairy-Free

Nut-Free

# Fully Loaded Grilled Caesar Salad

Serves 4

2 tablespoons extra-virgin olive oil

3 romaine hearts

Salt and freshly ground black pepper

2 boneless, skin-on chicken breasts (see Tip)

4 large hard-boiled eggs, peeled and halved lengthwise

2 cups halved cherry tomatoes

¼ small red onion, thinly sliced (about ¼ cup)

2 tablespoons capers, drained

⅓ cup Caesar Dressing (page 198)

I love taking old favorites and making them new again. Old-school Caesar salads are sooo 1976, you guys. Grilled Caesars with loads more toppings are where it's at. Feel free to add extra goodies like diced avocado, beets, or jicama to make it even more delicious. Bonus fun fact: Did you know Caesar Salad was rumored to have been first created in Tijuana, Mexico, in the 1920s? Truth.

Heat a grill to medium or heat a large grill pan over medium heat.

Lightly drizzle 1 tablespoon of the olive oil over the romaine hearts and season with a pinch each of salt and pepper.

Coat the chicken breasts with the remaining 1 tablespoon oil and season liberally with salt and pepper.

Place the romaine hearts and chicken breasts (skin-side down) on the grill or pan. Cook the lettuce until it's slightly softened and the edges are charred, 5 minutes. Cook the chicken breasts until they reach an internal temperature of 165°F, 6 to 7 minutes on each side. Remove both from the grill.

Let the chicken rest for 5 minutes, then slice it into ½-inch pieces. Slice the romaine hearts lengthwise into quarters.

Top the romaine segments with the sliced chicken and hard-boiled eggs, cherry tomatoes, red onion, and capers. Drizzle with the Caesar Dressing and serve immediately.

**Tip** *I always get my boneless, skin-on chicken breasts from the meat counter at my local grocery store, where they are happy to remove the bones for me (or you can remove them yourself at home). While I prefer to leave the skin on, this recipe will be just as delicious if you use boneless, skinless chicken breasts.*

Paleo

Whole30

Gluten-Free

Dairy-Free

Nut-Free

# Cauliflower + Pancetta Risott'no

**Serves 4 to 6**

10 cups cauliflower florets (about 2½ small heads)

3 garlic cloves, quartered

3 tablespoons unsalted butter or ghee (see Note)

3½ teaspoons salt, plus more to taste

12 ounces asparagus, chopped (about 1 cup)

3 tablespoons plus 1 teaspoon avocado oil or extra-virgin olive oil

½ pound pancetta, diced

1 medium sweet onion, diced (about 1 cup)

8 ounces sliced cremini mushrooms

1 teaspoon fresh lemon juice

1 teaspoon freshly ground black pepper

1 teaspoon chopped fresh thyme

My husband makes a mean traditional risotto—complete with all that signature butter and cheese. It's one of his specialties, and also one of my favorite dishes. Unfortunately, it leaves me in a major food coma, so we don't indulge in it too often. Instead, I came up with this grain- and dairy-free version, so I can indulge that craving without feeling weighed down.

Fill a medium stockpot with 3 inches of water. Set a steamer basket above the water and bring the water to a boil. Add 6 cups of the cauliflower florets and the garlic to the basket. Cover the pot and steam until the florets are tender but not soggy, about 7 minutes. Set the cauliflower and garlic aside to cool for 10 minutes. Do not drain the water from the stockpot. Place the remaining 4 cups cauliflower florets in a food processor and pulse until broken down to a rice-like consistency. Set aside.

Transfer the cooled cauliflower florets and garlic to a blender. Add the butter and ½ teaspoon of the salt and blend on high until smooth, about 30 seconds. Set aside.

Put the asparagus in the steamer basket and steam until tender, 3 to 4 minutes. Remove from the steamer basket and set aside.

In a large Dutch oven over medium heat, heat 1 teaspoon of the avocado oil. Add the pancetta, onion, and 1 teaspoon of the salt and cook, stirring frequently, until the onion is lightly browned and the pancetta is lightly crisped, 10 to 12 minutes. Remove from the heat and transfer to a large bowl.

In a large skillet over medium heat, heat 2 tablespoons of the oil. Add the mushrooms and ½ teaspoon of the salt. Cook, stirring frequently, until the mushrooms are tender and cooked through, 6 to 8 minutes. Use a slotted spoon to transfer the mushrooms to the bowl with the pancetta and onion.

In the Dutch oven over medium heat, heat the remaining 1 tablespoon oil. Add the cauliflower rice and remaining 1 teaspoon salt. Toss to coat. Cook, stirring, until the cauliflower rice is tender, 5 to 6 minutes. Add the cauliflower-garlic puree, asparagus, pancetta, onion, and mushrooms and stir to combine. Season with the lemon juice, pepper, and thyme. Stir to combine. Taste and season with salt.

**Note** *If you're doing a Whole30, make sure to use ghee instead of butter.*

Paleo

Whole30

Gluten-Free

Dairy-Free

Nut-Free

# Italian Spaghetti Squash

Serves 2 to 4

1 medium spaghetti squash, quartered and seeded (see Note)

3 tablespoons extra-virgin olive oil

1½ teaspoons salt

⅛ teaspoon freshly ground black pepper

2 scallions, sliced

1 large tomato, diced (about 1 cup)

2 garlic cloves, minced

⅛ teaspoon red pepper flakes

2 tablespoons chopped fresh basil

Is there anything that some fresh tomatoes, garlic, and basil can't make amazing? I think not. And this spaghetti squash is no exception.

Preheat the oven to 425°F. Line a baking sheet with parchment paper.

Drizzle each of the spaghetti squash quarters with ¾ teaspoon of the olive oil. Sprinkle with ½ teaspoon of the salt and the black pepper. Place the squash onto the baking sheet and roast for 35 minutes, or until it is fork-tender and the edges have lightly browned.

In a small skillet over medium-high heat, heat the remaining 2 tablespoons oil. Add the scallions and cook, stirring frequently, until tender and fragrant, 2 minutes. Add the tomato and ½ teaspoon of the salt to the pan and cook, stirring, until the tomato is heated through, 2 minutes more. Add the garlic and red pepper flakes and cook, stirring frequently to keep from burning the garlic, for 2 to 3 minutes more. Transfer to a large bowl and set aside.

When the spaghetti squash has finished roasting, let it cool for 5 minutes, then use a fork to scrape out the flesh into a large bowl. Toss the squash with the tomato sauce and the remaining ½ teaspoon salt.

Top with the basil and serve.

**Note** *As I've mentioned before, cutting a spaghetti squash is no easy feat. You can search online for a million ways to break into one, but here's how I do it: With a sharp knife, I slice the spaghetti squash lengthwise down the center, then place the halves cut-side down on the cutting board and cut them in half lengthwise to make four wedges. Use a spoon to scrape out the seeds.*

Paleo
Whole30
Gluten-Free
Vegan
Vegetarian
Dairy-Free
Nut-Free

# Roasted Eggplant Bake

**Serves 4**

2 medium globe eggplants (about 2 pounds), sliced into ½-inch-thick discs

2 tablespoons plus 2 teaspoons extra-virgin olive oil

3½ teaspoons salt

¼ teaspoon freshly ground black pepper

1 medium sweet onion, diced (about 1 cup)

4 garlic cloves, minced

1 (27-ounce) can crushed tomatoes

¼ cup chopped fresh basil

2 medium tomatoes, thinly sliced

1 cup crushed pork rinds (see Note)

8 ounces whole-milk mozzarella cheese, grated (see Note)

I've been making a version of this dish for the last ten years. As the years have gone by and I've altered my diet, the recipe has changed to reflect that. I've replaced the bread crumbs with pork rinds and reduced the cheese by a *lot*. Okay, okay, I lie—maybe by a quarter. What can I say? Cheese is my weakness! With or without a ton of cheesy goodness, my girls gobble this up. It's a great way to sneak in a veggie that they might not normally eat on its own.

Preheat the oven to 450°F. Line two large baking sheets with parchment paper.

Place the eggplant discs in an even layer on the prepared baking sheets and lightly coat with 2 tablespoons of the olive oil. Sprinkle with 1 teaspoon of the salt and the pepper. Roast for 20 minutes. Flip the discs and roast for 10 minutes more.

While the eggplant roasts, in a large skillet over medium heat, heat the remaining 2 teaspoons oil. Add the onion and ½ teaspoon of the salt and cook, stirring frequently, until the onion is tender and lightly browned, 7 to 9 minutes. Add the garlic and cook for 1 minute. Reduce the heat to medium-low, add the crushed tomatoes, basil, and remaining 2 teaspoons salt, and simmer for 2 minutes.

Remove the eggplant from the oven and reduce the oven temperature to 375°F.

Spread 1½ cups of the tomato sauce over the bottom of a 9 by 5-inch ceramic or nonstick loaf pan. Layer with one-third each of the eggplant, fresh tomato slices, pork rinds, and mozzarella. Repeat until you have three layers.

Bake for 25 minutes. Let cool for 5 minutes before serving. Slice into the bake and serve.

 **Note** *To modify for Paleo or Whole30, omit the mozzarella and pork rinds.*

Paleo if Modified

Whole30-Compliant If Modified

Gluten-Free

Nut-Free

# Crusty Cauliflower Bites

Serves 4

1 head cauliflower, cut into 1-inch
  florets (about 4 cups)

3 tablespoons salted butter
  or ghee, melted

½ cup crushed pork rinds (see Note)

2 tablespoons nutritional yeast

1 teaspoon lime zest

2 teaspoons fresh lime juice

1 teaspoon salt

1 teaspoon chili powder

4 lime wedges, for serving

When I make these, my kids chow down as if they haven't eaten all day. It's great, because they're eating their vegetables, but also bad, because *I* want in on the action, too. If they had it their way, they'd be eating the whole darn head of cauliflower themselves, but I can't say I blame them.

Preheat the oven to 425°F. Line a large baking sheet with parchment paper.

In a large bowl, combine the cauliflower florets and the melted butter and toss to coat completely. Add the pork rinds, nutritional yeast, lime zest, lemon juice, salt, and chili powder and stir until the mixture evenly coats the cauliflower.

Spread the cauliflower in an even layer on the prepared baking sheet. Roast for 25 minutes, or until it is tender and the edges are golden brown.

Serve with the lime wedges alongside for squeezing over top.

**Note** *To modify for Whole30 or vegetarians, omit the pork rinds.*

Paleo

Whole30-
Compliant If
Modified

Gluten-Free

Vegetarian
If Modified

Dairy-Free

Nut-Free

# Creamy Spinach + Sweet Potato Swoodles

## Serves 4

2½ tablespoons extra-virgin olive or avocado oil

5 garlic cloves, coarsely chopped

1 cup raw cashews, soaked in ½ cup water for 3 hours and drained

¼ cup unsweetened almond milk

Salt and freshly ground black pepper

Pinch of ground nutmeg

2 cups halved cherry tomatoes

½ cup chopped white onion (about ½ medium)

6 cups baby spinach

2 pounds sweet potatoes (about 2 large), peeled and spiralized (see Note)

Red pepper flakes (optional)

I have to confess, I've never been a huge pasta fan, unless it was stuffed with cheese and meat and slathered in a heavy sauce. I mean, who *doesn't* love that? However, I can most definitely get behind sweet potato "pasta." I love the mild sweet flavor the sweet potato brings and the variety of ways you can serve the "noodles." As always, feel free to mix up the veggies in this dish. Get creative and swap in some kale or bok choy for the spinach. You can also add some roasted chicken or shrimp for more protein.

In a medium skillet over medium heat, heat 1 tablespoon of the olive oil. Add the garlic and cook, stirring, until tender, 1 to 2 minutes. Use a slotted spoon to remove the garlic from the pan, leaving the oil behind.

In a blender or food processor, combine the cashews and garlic. Add ½ cup water, the almond milk, ½ teaspoon salt, ½ teaspoon black pepper, and the nutmeg and blend until smooth. Set aside.

Add the cherry tomatoes to the same pan you used for the garlic and set over medium-high heat. Cook, without stirring, until the heat begins to blister the skin, 2 to 3 minutes. Reduce the heat to medium and add the onion. Cook, stirring, until the onion is tender and lightly browned, 5 to 7 minutes. Add the spinach, along with an additional ½ tablespoon of the oil if the pan looks dry. Cook, stirring, until the spinach wilts, 3 to 4 minutes. Remove from the heat.

In a large bowl, toss the spiralized sweet potato noodles with the remaining 1 tablespoon oil and season with a pinch each of salt and black pepper.

In a large skillet or Dutch oven over medium heat, cook the sweet potato noodles, stirring frequently, until tender, 7 to 10 minutes. Add the spinach mixture and the cashew cream, stir to coat, and cook until the sweet potatoes are heated through, 8 to 10 minutes.

Sprinkle with red pepper flakes for a touch of heat, if desired, and serve immediately.

**Tip** *When you're making your swoodles, spiralize a couple of extra sweet potatoes and store those noodles in the fridge for the week. Having them on hand will make weeknight dinners and breakfasts extra easy.*

Paleo

Whole30

Gluten-Free

Vegan

Vegetarian

Dairy-Free

# Salt + Vinegar Kale Chips

Serves 2 to 4

2 tablespoons white wine vinegar

1½ tablespoons extra-virgin olive oil

1 teaspoon flaky sea salt
(I like Maldon)

1 bunch red or lacinato kale

Salt-and-vinegar potato chips are my all-time favorite, so when I discovered that I could replicate them with kale, I was ecstatic. When it comes to making kale chips, you can either remove the ribs before or after roasting them. The rib keeps the kale leaf from lying flat on the pan as it bakes and allows a little more airflow to help crisp them.

Preheat the oven to 425°F. Line two large baking sheets with parchment paper.

In a large bowl, whisk together the vinegar, olive oil, and salt. Lightly dip each kale leaf into the mixture and massage the leaf to coat. Place the leaves in an even layer without overlapping them on the prepared baking sheets and bake for 10 minutes, until crispy. Enjoy immediately.

Paleo

Whole30

Gluten-Free

Vegan

Vegetarian

Dairy-Free

Nut-Free

# Beets with Honey + Pistachios

## Serves 4

6 medium mixed red and golden beets, scrubbed

1 teaspoon extra-virgin olive oil

¼ cup crumbled goat cheese

2 tablespoons shelled pistachios, chopped

2 teaspoons chopped fresh thyme

½ teaspoon salt

1 tablespoon honey

This recipe is a great example of my own personal Food Freedom. While I don't include dairy and sugars in my diet in quite the same way that I did fifteen years ago, they're still there. I use ingredients like goat cheese and honey in small amounts I can tolerate and pair them with healthier foods, like these roasted fresh beets. It makes for a dish that feels healthy and indulgent at the same time.

Preheat the oven to 400°F. Line a large rimmed baking sheet with aluminum foil.

Toss the beets with the olive oil and wrap each beet with a piece of aluminum foil. Place on the prepared baking sheet and roast for 50 minutes to 1 hour, until the beets are fork-tender. Let cool for 10 minutes, or until cool enough to handle. Peel the cooled beets and slice them into wedges.

Put the beets in a large serving bowl. Sprinkle with the goat cheese, pistachios, thyme, and salt, drizzle with the honey, and serve.

Gluten-Free

Vegetarian

# Soups, Stews + Chili, Too

GREAT FOR LEFTOVERS!
★ ★ ★

# Green Curry Sweet Potato Soup

### Serves 4

2 medium sweet potatoes, peeled and cut into bite-size cubes

1 tablespoon extra-virgin olive oil

½ teaspoon smoked paprika

½ teaspoon salt

2 (32-ounce) containers salted chicken broth

2 (15-ounce) cans full-fat coconut milk

8 ounces green curry paste

1 (2-inch) piece fresh ginger, peeled and very thinly sliced

2 tablespoons coconut aminos

2 tablespoons honey (see Note)

1 tablespoon fish sauce

3 cups sliced cremini mushrooms (about 6 ounces)

1 red bell pepper, thinly sliced

½ medium yellow onion, thinly sliced (about ½ cup)

2½ pounds boneless, skinless chicken breasts, thinly sliced across the grain (see Tip)

½ cup chopped fresh basil, for serving

Lime wedges, for serving

Of all the curries, green curry has always been my favorite. I love how it's just the tiniest bit sweet— but I don't love how it's usually made with sugar. I cut back on that sweetness in this dish by using only a little honey and instead relying on sweet potatoes to give it a similar flavor profile. Score! A perfectly balanced green curry flavor without a lot of additional sugar.

Preheat the oven to 425°F. Line a baking sheet with parchment paper.

In a large bowl, combine the sweet potatoes, olive oil, paprika, and salt and toss to coat. Divide the potatoes between the prepared baking sheets and arrange them in an even layer. Roast for 25 to 30 minutes, until tender and golden brown.

In a large stockpot over medium heat, combine the broth, coconut milk, curry paste, ginger, coconut aminos, honey, and fish sauce. Stir to combine. Add the mushrooms, bell pepper, and onion to the pot and bring to a boil. Add the chicken. Reduce the heat to medium and simmer for 10 minutes more. Add the sweet potatoes, taste, and season with salt.

Top with the chopped basil. Serve with lime wedges alongside for squeezing over top.

**Note** *To modify for Whole30, omit the honey.*

**Tip** *To thinly slice your chicken breasts with ease, partially freeze them prior to slicing. It's okay to add them to the soup while they're still slightly frozen; they'll cook up just as well!*

Paleo

Whole30-Compliant If Modified

Gluten-Free

Dairy-Free

Nut-Free

# Pho-Style Asian Chicken Zoodle Soup

Serves 4

8 cups Homemade Bone Broth
(page 182), or 2 (32-ounce) containers
salted chicken broth

1 (3-inch) piece fresh ginger,
peeled and finely grated

2 tablespoons fish sauce

1 tablespoon coconut aminos

1½ teaspoons fresh lime juice
(from 1 lime)

5 scallions, sliced

1 teaspoon salt

1½ pounds boneless, skinless
chicken breasts, thinly sliced
(see Tip, page 169)

4 ounces cremini mushrooms, sliced

2 cups chopped lacinato kale
(about ½ bunch)

1 medium zucchini, spiralized using
a medium blade

⅓ cup chopped fresh cilantro,
plus more for garnish

2 cups mung bean sprouts

1 jalapeño, sliced

8 to 12 fresh mint leaves

4 soft-boiled large eggs, peeled
and halved lengthwise

While I love the flavors of pho, making a traditional version can be time-consuming and, more than often, use ingredients that leave me feeling lousy. Because of that, I took all the flavors that I've come to love in pho and added them to a frothy soup that can be made even on the busiest of evenings. A faux pho, if you will.

In a large stockpot, combine the broth, ginger, fish sauce, coconut aminos, lime juice, one-third of the scallions, and the salt and bring to a boil. Reduce the heat to maintain a simmer and cook, uncovered, for 10 minutes. Add the chicken and mushrooms and simmer until the mushrooms are tender and the chicken is cooked through, 5 to 7 minutes. Add the kale and zucchini and cook until tender, 3 to 4 minutes. Add the cilantro and remove from the heat.

Divide the soup among four serving bowls and top each with ¼ cup of the mung bean sprouts, 2 or 3 jalapeño slices, 2 or 3 mint leaves, additional cilantro, and 2 soft-boiled egg halves.

Paleo

Whole30

Gluten-Free

Dairy-Free

Nut-Free

# Pizza Soup

My husband, Brad, looked at me like I was crazy when I told him that I put this recipe in the book. "Doesn't that sound a bit . . . *pedestrian*?" he asked. \*☺.\* I'm not sure when he became such a food snob, but I clearly need to stop feeding him so well. It's okay, though, because I knew I was in for a big "I told you so" moment when I perfected the soup and let Brad try it. He loved it, and I was completely vindicated. So, Brad, this recipe is dedicated to you and your finely tuned, too-cool-for-school palate.

**Serves 4**

1½ medium yellow onions

2½ pounds medium tomatoes, quartered

4 garlic cloves, quartered

2 tablespoons plus 1 teaspoon extra-virgin olive oil

3 teaspoons salt

1 pound mild Italian sausage, casings removed (see Tip)

1 green bell pepper, diced

1 (32-ounce) container salted chicken broth

2 tablespoons tomato paste

1 teaspoon dried oregano

½ teaspoon dried parsley

½ teaspoon freshly ground black pepper

⅓ cup chopped fresh basil, plus more for garnish

1 (2.25-ounce) can sliced pitted black olives (about ¼ cup), drained

Red pepper flakes, for serving

Preheat the oven to 450°F. Line a large baking sheet with parchment paper.

Quarter one of the onions and finely chop the remaining ½ onion.

In a large bowl, combine the quartered onion, tomatoes, garlic, 2 tablespoons of the olive oil, and 1 teaspoon of the salt and toss to coat. Spread the ingredients in an even layer on the prepared baking sheet and roast for 35 minutes, or until the onion is tender and golden on the edges.

While the tomatoes and onion roast, in a large skillet over medium heat, heat the remaining 1 teaspoon oil. Add the sausage and cook, gently breaking up the meat with a wooden spoon and stirring frequently, until cooked through, 5 to 6 minutes. Remove the sausage from the pan and transfer to paper towels to drain. Set aside.

Add the finely chopped onion to the same pan and cook, stirring frequently, until the onion is tender and lightly caramelized, 6 to 7 minutes. Add the bell pepper and cook, stirring, until softened, 4 to 5 minutes.

In a large stockpot over medium heat, combine the roasted tomatoes and onion, the broth, tomato paste, oregano, parsley, black pepper, and remaining 2 teaspoons salt. Using an immersion blender, blend the soup until well incorporated. (If you don't have an immersion blender, you can carefully transfer the mixture to a standing blender, let cool briefly, carefully puree, and pour the soup back into the pot.) Bring the soup to a boil, then reduce the heat to low and return the cooked sausage and vegetables to the pot. Simmer for 5 to 7 minutes, then add the basil and olives. Remove from the heat.

Top with additional basil and red pepper flakes and serve.

**Tip** *Make sure to check the ingredients in your sausage. If you cannot find a Whole30 compliant sausage, regular ground pork will be just as tasty.*

Paleo

Whole30

Gluten-Free

Dairy-Free

Nut-Free

# Spicy Pork + Kale Soup

## Serves 4 to 6

2 teaspoons avocado oil
or extra-virgin olive oil

1 pound spicy Italian sausage, casings
removed (see Tip)

8 ounces sliced cremini mushrooms

3 teaspoons salt

2 (32-ounce) containers unsalted
chicken broth

6 cups chopped lacinato kale,
leaves only (about 1 bunch)

2 scallions, chopped

¼ cup coconut aminos

1 teaspoon toasted sesame oil

2 garlic cloves, minced

1 (1-inch) piece fresh ginger,
peeled and finely grated

1 cup mung bean sprouts, for garnish

⅓ cup chopped fresh cilantro,
for garnish

I'm always down for mixing flavors from different cuisines to make something delicious. And when spicy Italian sausage, sesame oil, and kale meet, good things happen. If you're looking to make this Whole30-compliant, simply swap out the Italian sausage for ground pork and red pepper flakes or make sure the sausage is compliant.

In a large skillet over medium heat, heat 1 teaspoon of the avocado oil. Add the sausage and cook, using a spatula to gently break it into small, bite-size pieces, until the sausage is lightly browned and cooked through, 5 to 6 minutes. Use a slotted spoon to transfer the sausage to a bowl or plate and set aside.

In the same pan, heat the remaining 1 teaspoon avocado oil. Add the mushrooms and 1 teaspoon of the salt. Cook, stirring, until the mushrooms until tender, 5 to 6 minutes.

Pour the broth into a large stockpot over high heat. Stir in the cooked sausage, mushrooms, kale, scallions, coconut aminos, sesame oil, garlic, ginger, and remaining 2 teaspoons salt and bring to a boil. Reduce the heat to maintain a simmer and cook for 10 minutes.

To serve, ladle into bowls and top each with a pinch each of the mung bean sprouts and cilantro.

> **Tip** *Make sure to check the ingredients in your sausage. If you cannot find a Whole30 compliant sausage, regular ground pork with a pinch of red pepper flakes will be just as tasty.*

Whole30
Gluten-Free
Vegan
Vegetarian
Dairy-Free
Nut-Free

GREAT FOR LEFTOVERS!

# Carrot, Ginger + Turmeric Soup

**Serves 4**

6 cups baby carrots

1 cup coarsely chopped yellow onion (about 1 medium)

2 tablespoons extra-virgin olive oil

3 teaspoons salt

½ teaspoon freshly ground black pepper

4 garlic cloves, coarsely chopped

1 (32-ounce) container unsalted chicken or vegetable broth (see Tip)

½ cup full-fat coconut milk

1 (3-inch) piece fresh turmeric, peeled and finely grated

1 (2-inch) piece fresh ginger, peeled and finely grated

Spiralized or shredded carrot, for garnish (optional)

Fun fact: Every time I make a soup, I sing to myself, "Soup, soup-aloup, soup-aloup-aloup-aloup" to the tune of a popular '90s R&B song (any guesses on that one?).

But I digress.

Vegetable soups are such a quick and easy way to load up on nutrients. I added some turmeric and ginger to this one not just for the added health benefits, but to kick the flavor up a notch. I also use baby carrots since they come pre-peeled and -chopped. During a busy week, I'll take all the extra help I can get! There ain't no shame in it. To add some protein, feel free to top your soup with a fried egg or two.

Preheat the oven to 400°F.

In a large bowl, combine the carrots, onion, olive oil, and 1 teaspoon of the salt and toss to coat.

Divide the mixture between two 9 by 13-inch baking dishes and roast for 20 minutes. Add the garlic and flip the vegetables, then roast for 20 minutes more, or until the vegetables are softened and lightly browned.

Transfer the roasted vegetables to a blender, add the broth, and blend on high for 1 minute, or until the mixture is completely smooth.

Transfer the puree to a large stockpot over medium heat. Stir in the coconut milk, turmeric, ginger, and remaining 2 teaspoons salt. Bring to a simmer and cook for 15 minutes prior to serving. Serve hot, garnished with carrot, if desired..

**Tip** ▶ *Make sure to use vegetable broth in lieu of chicken broth if you want to make this vegetarian or vegan.*

Paleo

Whole30

Vegetarian

Vegan

Dairy-Free

Nut-Free

# Loaded Lentil Soup

## Serves 6

1 teaspoon extra-virgin olive oil

1 cup diced pancetta (about 4 ounces)

2 medium yellow onions, diced (about 2 cups)

2 carrots, finely chopped

3 celery stalks, chopped

2 garlic cloves, minced

2 (32-ounce) containers salted chicken broth

1 cup green lentils, rinsed

1 (14.5-ounce) can diced tomatoes

1½ teaspoons chopped fresh thyme

1 bay leaf

¼ medium head cauliflower, cut into florets, or 1 cup store-bought cauliflower rice

4 cups chopped lacinato kale, leaves only (about ½ bunch)

2 teaspoons salt

¼ teaspoon freshly ground black pepper

While I love a hearty lentil soup, this version is lighter on the lentils and heavier on the veggies. For some extra bulk and a boost of nutrients, I add kale and cauliflower rice. You get all the flavors of a traditional lentil soup with a lot more nutritional bang for your buck.

In a large Dutch oven or stockpot over medium heat, heat the olive oil. Add the pancetta and cook, stirring occasionally, until the pancetta has rendered down and is lightly golden around the edges, 3 to 4 minutes. Add the onion and cook, stirring occasionally, until tender and translucent, 5 to 6 minutes. Add the carrots and celery and cook, stirring occasionally, until tender, about 5 minutes. Add the garlic and cook, stirring frequently, until fragrant, 1 minute. Stir in the broth, lentils, tomatoes, thyme, and bay leaf and bring to a boil. Cover the pot and reduce the heat to maintain a simmer. Simmer for 50 minutes. Remove and discard the bay leaf.

While the soup simmers, if using fresh cauliflower, in a food processor, pulse the florets until broken down to a rice-like consistency. (Skip this step if using store-bought cauliflower rice.) Set aside.

Carefully transfer 2 cups of the soup to a blender. Blend on high for 10 seconds, then return the soup to the pot. Add the kale, cauliflower rice, salt, and pepper and simmer for 10 minutes.

Serve hot.

Gluten-Free
Dairy-Free
Nut-Free

# Dairy-Free Cream of Mushroom Soup

## Serves 4

2½ tablespoons extra-virgin olive oil

2 pounds cremini mushrooms, sliced

2 teaspoons salt

3 garlic cloves, minced

½ medium white onion, chopped (about ½ cup)

1 (32-ounce) container unsalted chicken or vegetable broth

½ cup full-fat coconut milk, plus extra for swirling

1 tablespoon fish sauce

2 teaspoons coconut aminos

2 teaspoons chopped fresh thyme, plus sprigs for garnish

1 teaspoon chopped fresh rosemary

1 bay leaf

1 tablespoon arrowroot powder

I used to make a version of this soup for Thanksgiving every year, but *that* version was loaded with tons of heavy cream and butter. It was delicious, but I can't say it made a great everyday soup. Special occasion? Sure. Wednesday-night dinner? Probably not. That's why I developed this cleaned-up version. It's made without all the unnecessary cream and butter of the original, but tastes just as delicious. A friend even tried it and said she couldn't believe it was actually healthy!

In a large skillet over medium heat, heat 2 tablespoons of the olive oil. Add the mushrooms and salt and stir to coat with the olive oil. Cook, stirring occasionally, until the mushrooms are tender and have released most of their moisture, 9 to 12 minutes. Add the garlic and cook, stirring constantly, until fragrant, 1 minute. Set aside.

In a large stockpot over medium heat, heat the remaining ½ tablespoon oil. Add the onion and cook, stirring occasionally, until tender and translucent, 7 to 9 minutes. Add the mushrooms, broth, coconut milk, fish sauce, coconut aminos, thyme, rosemary, and bay leaf and bring to a boil. Reduce the heat to maintain a simmer. Remove and discard the bay leaf. Using a handheld mixer or immersion blender, blend the soup for 10 to 15 seconds. It should retain some texture and not be perfectly smooth.

In a small bowl, mix together the arrowroot powder and 1 tablespoon water. While stirring, slowly drizzle the arrowroot mixture into the soup. Simmer for 2 minutes more until thickened.

To serve, drizzle each serving with a small amount of coconut milk and gently swirl it with a spoon. Garnish with fresh thyme sprigs.

**Note** *For a vegan or vegetarian version of this soup, be sure to use vegetable broth and omit the fish sauce.*

Paleo

Whole30

Gluten-Free

Dairy-Free

Nut-Free

# Homemade Chicken Bone Broth

Makes about 7 cups

3 pounds chicken bones (see Tip)

2 medium carrots

3 celery stalks

1 large yellow onion, quartered

3 garlic cloves, smashed

2 sprigs fresh thyme

1 sprig fresh rosemary

2 teaspoons salt

1 teaspoon whole black peppercorns

1 tablespoon apple cider vinegar

Each winter we guzzle loads of homemade bone broth, and I swear it keeps those nasty winter germs at bay. We drink it so much that my kiddos have affectionately started calling it "chicken tea," which I guess it kind of is. While you can buy bone broth readily at the store these days, making your own at home is quite easy and incredibly cost effective. Feel free to use this aromatic broth as a base for soups or just to sip on. Salt to taste if you are planning to drink as a beverage.

**To cook on the stovetop:**
Put all the ingredients in an 8-quart (or larger) stockpot with 8 cups water and bring the water to a boil. Reduce the heat to low and simmer, partially covered, for 8 hours.

Remove the solid ingredients from the pot and pour the broth through a fine-mesh strainer to remove any smaller bits.

**To cook in a slow cooker:**
Put all the ingredients in a slow cooker with 8 cups water. Cover and cook on Low for 10 to 12 hours.

Remove the solid ingredients from the slow cooker and pour the broth through a fine-mesh strainer to remove any smaller bits.

**To cook in an Instant Pot:**
Put all the ingredients in an Instant Pot with 8 cups water. Cover and set the Instant Pot to manual for 2 hours. Allow the Instant Pot to release pressure naturally.

Paleo

Whole30

Gluten-Free

Dairy-Free

Nut-Free

Remove the solid ingredients from the Instant Pot and pour the broth through a fine-mesh strainer to remove any smaller bits.

Store the broth in an airtight container in the refrigerator for up to 1 week or pour into a freeze-proof container and store for up to 3 months.

**Tip** *Once the broth has cooled in the refrigerator, the fat will solidify at the top and you can easily scoop it off. (I like to leave a little bit behind for additional flavor.)*

**Tip** *You can either reserve leftover chicken bones from your own kitchen or purchase chicken bones from the meat counter at your grocery store or butcher. We freeze any leftover chicken bones, so I always have a stash on hand.*

# Sweet Potato + Chocolate Chili

**Serves 6**

2 medium sweet potatoes, peeled and cut into bite-size cubes

1 tablespoon plus 1 teaspoon extra-virgin olive oil

3 teaspoons salt

3 bacon slices, chopped

2 medium yellow onions, diced (about 2 cups)

5 garlic cloves, minced

2 red bell peppers, diced

2½ pounds 85% lean ground beef

2 tablespoons chili powder

1 tablespoon ground cumin

1 tablespoon smoked paprika

1 tablespoon coconut aminos

1 teaspoon freshly ground black pepper

1 teaspoon red pepper flakes

⅓ cup semisweet chocolate morsels, or 2 tablespoons unsweetened cocoa powder (see Note)

1 (15-ounce) can diced tomatoes

1 (15-ounce) can tomato sauce

1 (12-ounce) bottle gluten-free beer (I like a lager), or 2 cups chicken broth (see Note)

I started making a chocolate and sweet potato chili long before I ever decided to clean up my diet. Back then, I used hot chocolate packets (what?!) instead of the semisweet chocolate morsels I use now. It's not just the chocolate that's changed, though; I swap out gluten-y stout for gluten-free lager and throw in some sweet potato chunks instead of beans. Those ingredients, along with some tomatoes and beef, strike a perfect balance between sweet and savory and make for a chili that stands up to any traditional version.

Preheat the oven to 350°F. Line two large baking sheets with parchment paper.

In a large bowl, toss together the sweet potatoes, 1 tablespoon of the olive oil, and 1 teaspoon of the salt. Spread the sweet potatoes in an even layer over the prepared baking sheets. Roast for 35 minutes, or until the sweet potatoes are tender and golden brown around the edges. Set aside.

In a large Dutch oven or stockpot over medium heat, cook the bacon, stirring occasionally, until just beginning to render its fat, 4 to 5 minutes. Add the onion and cook, stirring occasionally, until tender, 6 to 7 minutes. Add the garlic and cook, stirring, until fragrant, 1 minute. Stir in the bell peppers and cook, stirring occasionally, for 2 minutes.

Push the ingredients to one side of the pan and add the remaining 1 teaspoon oil to the other side. Add the ground beef and cook, gently breaking it up with a wooden spoon or spatula. Stir in the chili powder, cumin, paprika, coconut aminos, black pepper, red pepper flakes, and 1 teaspoon of the salt. Cook, stirring occasionally, until the ground beef is cooked through, 6 to 7 minutes. Add the chocolate and stir to combine. Pour in the diced tomatoes, tomato sauce, and beer. Add the remaining 1 teaspoon salt and bring to a simmer. Simmer for 10 minutes. Add the roasted sweet potatoes and simmer for 10 minutes more.

**Note** ▸ *If you're doing a Whole30, be sure to use cocoa powder instead of chocolate morsels and chicken broth instead of beer.*

Paleo

Whole30-Compliant If Modified

Gluten-Free

Dairy-Free

Nut-Free

# Ropa Vieja

*Ropa vieja* is a traditional Cuban dish made with stewed beef and vegetables. It quite literally means "old clothes." But trust me, it tastes far superior to anything you might find in your hamper. There's no limit to the ways you can enjoy this dish, which is fantastic, because you'll have plenty of leftovers. Try it over a bed of cauliflower rice, on a baked potato, or with Cool-er Ranch Plantains (page 47).

### Serves 6

2 pounds flank steak

3 teaspoons salt

1 (14.5-ounce) can crushed tomatoes

½ cup unsalted beef broth or chicken broth

1 (6-ounce) can tomato paste

2 teaspoons smoked paprika

1 teaspoon ground cumin

½ teaspoon ground allspice

½ teaspoon whole black peppercorns

½ teaspoon freshly ground black pepper

1 medium yellow onion, halved and sliced (about 1 cup)

1 red bell pepper, sliced

1 green bell pepper, sliced

5 garlic cloves, minced

Cauliflower rice or potatoes, for serving

⅓ cup chopped fresh cilantro, for serving

Season both sides of the flank steak with 2 teaspoons of the salt.

In a slow cooker or Instant Pot, combine the crushed tomatoes, broth, tomato paste, paprika, cumin, allspice, peppercorns, black pepper, and remaining 1 teaspoon salt. Stir, then add the onion, bell peppers, and garlic. Stir again to coat. Add the flank steak and cover with half the vegetable mixture.

If using a slow cooker, cover and cook on High for 5 hours. If using an Instant Pot, set to "Meat/Stew" and cook on high pressure for 1 hour 15 minutes. Let the Instant Pot release pressure naturally. Once cooked, shred the meat with a fork.

Serve over cauliflower rice or potatoes, garnished with the cilantro.

Paleo

Whole30

Gluten-Free

Dairy-Free

Nut-Free

# Split Pea + Crispy Prosciutto Soup

Serves 4

5 bacon slices, cut crosswise
into ¼-inch-wide pieces

1 cup chopped sweet onion
(about 1 medium)

¾ cup chopped carrots
(about 2 medium)

2 celery stalks, chopped

1 teaspoon salt

2 garlic cloves, minced

2 (32-ounce) containers unsalted
chicken broth

2 cups green split peas

8 slices prosciutto, cut in half

4 cups baby spinach

¼ teaspoon freshly ground
black pepper

Nothing beats a hearty one-pot soup that requires minimal dishwashing, and this soup is just that. Easy, delicious, and a light cleanup? I'm all in. While traditional split pea soup calls for a ham bone, I don't usually have a spare one lying around. Instead, I throw some bacon and prosciutto into the soup to bring the pork flavor, and indeed they do!

In a large stockpot over medium heat, cook the bacon, stirring occasionally, until lightly crisped, 6 to 7 minutes. Use a slotted spoon to transfer the bacon to a paper towel–lined plate to drain.

Add the onion, carrots, celery, and ½ teaspoon of the salt to the pot with the bacon drippings. Cook, stirring occasionally, until the vegetables have softened, 6 to 7 minutes. Add the garlic and cook, stirring frequently, until just softened, 1 minute. Add the broth and split peas. Bring to a low boil, cover, and cook, stirring occasionally, for 1 hour.

Meanwhile, preheat the oven to 350°F. Line a large baking sheet with parchment paper.

Lay the prosciutto slices in a single layer on the prepared baking sheet. Bake until crispy, 1 to 2 minutes. Transfer the slices to a wire rack to cool.

When the soup has cooked for about 1 hour, carefully transfer half the soup to a blender and let cool briefly. Add the spinach and blend on high for 20 to 30 seconds, until completely smooth. Pour the soup back into the pot and add 1½ cups water. Bring the soup to a simmer and season with the pepper and remaining ½ teaspoon salt. Cook for 10 minutes more.

Divide the soup among six bowls and top each serving with 1 or 2 prosciutto crisps.

Gluten-Free
Dairy-Free
Nut-Free

GREAT FOR LEFTOVERS!
★ ★ ★

# Turkey + Ancho Chile Soup

## Serves 4

2 teaspoons extra-virgin olive oil

1 pound 85% lean ground turkey

1 teaspoon salt

2 medium red onions, diced (about 2 cups)

1 red bell pepper, diced

1 teaspoon chili powder

1 teaspoon smoked paprika

½ teaspoon ground chipotle

3 garlic cloves, minced

1 (32-ounce) container salted chicken broth

1 cup canned diced tomatoes

8 small tomatillos, rinsed well and quartered

1 (4-ounce) can mild green chiles

3 dried ancho chiles, trimmed and quartered

2 tablespoons fresh lime juice (from about 1 lime)

½ cup chopped fresh cilantro, plus more for garnish

⅓ cup crumbled queso fresco (see Note)

⅓ cup crushed store-bought plantain chips (see Note)

¼ cup pepitas (pumpkin seeds)

This soup packs a mad punch of flavor. In case you didn't know, an ancho chile is simply a dried poblano pepper. It breaks down into the soup and adds a ton of flavor but not too much heat. Still, there is a decent kick to this recipe, so you may want to halve the spices if you're making it for the kids or prefer a milder version for yourself.

In a large stockpot or Dutch oven over medium-high heat, heat 1 teaspoon of the olive oil. Add the ground turkey and salt and cook, breaking up the turkey with a wooden spoon, until cooked through and lightly browned, 5 to 6 minutes. Using a slotted spoon, transfer the turkey to a paper towel–lined plate.

Reduce the heat to medium and add the remaining 1 teaspoon oil and the onion to the pot. Cook until translucent, 2 to 3 minutes. Add the bell pepper, chili powder, paprika, and chipotle and stir. Cook until the onion and bell pepper are tender, 5 to 6 minutes. Add the garlic and cook, stirring frequently, until fragrant, 1 minute. Increase the heat to medium-high and add the broth, tomatoes, tomatillos, green chiles, ancho chiles, and lime juice. Cover the pot and bring the soup to a low boil. Cook, stirring occasionally, for 12 minutes.

Reduce the heat to medium and simmer the soup until it develops a deep red color and the ancho chiles and tomatillos have broken down, 5 to 8 minutes. Stir in the cilantro and remove from the heat.

Top with the queso fresco, plantain chips, and pepitas and serve.

**Note** *To modify for Whole30, omit the queso fresco and plantain chips.*

Paleo

Whole30-Compliant If Modified

Gluten-Free

Dairy-Free

Nut-Free

# Condiments, Sauces + Dressings

# 1-Minute Mayonnaise

Makes 1 generous cup

1 cup extra-light-tasting olive oil
(I like Bel'Olio)

1 large egg

1 teaspoon Dijon mustard

½ teaspoon fresh lemon juice

¼ teaspoon salt

Holy moly, if I could call out any recipe in this book as a #gamechanger, this would be it. Most people are familiar with the drip method of making mayonnaise, but there's a better, more efficient way. And this is it. If you're as impatient as I am, this recipe is a godsend. But first, two things to note: 1) You will need a tall, wide-mouth mason jar or a comparable container that will fit an immersion blender; 2) Make sure to use extra-light-*tasting* olive oil as your base. Otherwise, you will end up with a pungent mess of a mayonnaise.

In a tall, wide-mouth mason jar or similar container, combine the olive oil, egg, Dijon mustard, lemon juice, and salt. Let the ingredients settle for a moment.

Place an immersion blender directly over the egg and begin to blend. Leave the blender in place for 5 seconds as the oil and egg begin to emulsify, then start to very slowly move the blender up and down until the oil and egg are fully emulsified, about 30 seconds. Cover and store in the refrigerator for up to 1 week.

Paleo

Whole30

Gluten-Free

Vegetarian

Dairy-Free

# Ranch Vinaigrette

Makes about ½ cup

½ cup extra-virgin olive oil

2 tablespoons white wine vinegar

1 tablespoon chopped fresh parsley

2 teaspoons chopped fresh dill

2 teaspoons chopped fresh chives

1 teaspoon minced red onion

1 garlic clove, minced

1 teaspoon salt

If you love a creamy ranch dressing, you're going to love this version just as much. It's zesty, it's herby, it's perfect. This works well on just about any salad or as a marinade for proteins like fish and chicken.

In a medium bowl, whisk together the oil, vinegar, parsley, dill, chives, onion, garlic, and salt. Use immediately or cover and store in the refrigerator for up to 3 days.

Paleo

Whole30

Vegan

Vegetarian

Gluten-Free

Dairy-Free

Nut-Free

# Caesar Dressing

Makes about ¾ cup

6 anchovy fillets packed in olive oil, drained

2 garlic cloves

2 tablespoons fresh lemon juice

1 teaspoon capers, drained

1 teaspoon Dijon mustard

¼ teaspoon lemon pepper

2 large egg yolks

½ cup extra-light-tasting olive oil (I like Bel'Olio)

One of my favorite salads will always be a Caesar salad, but store-bought Caesar dressing can be so disappointing. So I make my own. It works great on Caesar salad, of course, but also tastes amazing on tuna salad, grilled salmon, and chopped chicken salad. Oh, and don't let the anchovies freak you out—you truly won't notice them, and they're the key to replicating the Caesar dressing flavor we've come to know and love.

In a blender, combine the anchovies, garlic, lemon juice, capers, mustard, and lemon pepper and pulse until the mixture has broken down into a paste. Add the egg yolks and blend on medium speed until the egg is well incorporated. With the blender running on low speed, very slowly stream in the olive oil until the mixture emulsifies. The slower you stream in the oil, the better and creamier the results will be. Use immediately or cover and store in the refrigerator for up to 3 days.

Paleo

Whole30

Gluten-Free

Dairy-Free

Nut-Free

# Awesome Sauce

Makes ¾ cup

½ cup 1-Minute Mayonnaise
(page 195)

2 tablespoons tomato paste

2 teaspoons prepared horseradish

½ teaspoon all-purpose seasoning
(I like Trader Joe's 21 Seasoning
Salute or Mrs. Dash Original Blend)

¼ teaspoon salt

I mean, what more can you say about a sauce called "Awesome Sauce" than that it's awesome? Now go make it.

In a medium bowl, thoroughly combine the mayonnaise, tomato paste, horseradish, all-purpose seasoning, and salt. Use immediately or cover and store in the refrigerator for up to 1 week.

Paleo

Whole30

Gluten-Free

Vegetarian

Dairy-Free

Nut-Free

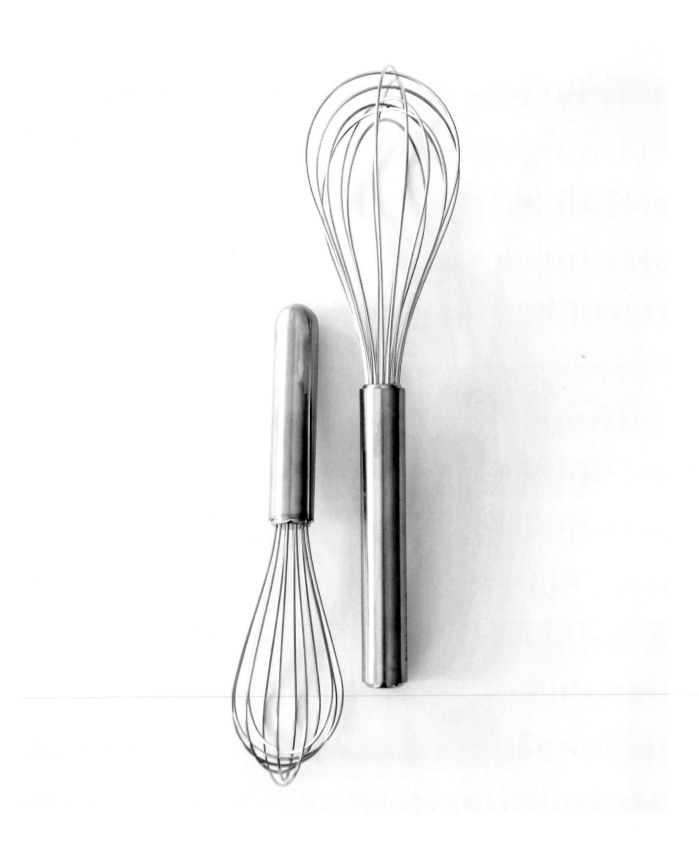

# Mustard-Maple Vinaigrette

Makes about ⅓ cup

¼ cup plus 2 tablespoons
extra-virgin olive oil

1 tablespoon white wine vinegar

1 tablespoon Dijon mustard

1½ teaspoons pure maple syrup

½ teaspoon salt

I love this dressing on dark-leafy-green salads. The flavors in it are bold enough to stand up to the heartiness of greens like kale or chard but not so overpowering that you won't taste the other ingredients.

In a medium bowl, thoroughly whisk together the olive oil, vinegar, mustard, maple syrup, and salt. Use immediately or cover and store in the refrigerator for 4 to 5 days.

Vegan

Vegetarian

Nut-Free

Gluten-Free

Dairy-Free

# Gremolata 2.0

4 garlic cloves, minced

⅓ cup crushed pistachios

¼ cup finely chopped fresh parsley

¼ cup finely chopped fresh cilantro

3 tablespoons extra-virgin olive oil

½ teaspoon salt

1 tablespoon grated lemon zest

¼ teaspoon fresh lemon juice

Pinch of red pepper flakes

Gremolata is a zesty, herby Italian condiment that you can use on all sorts of dishes, from fish to vegetables. Although gremolata is traditionally made using a combination of lemon, parsley, and garlic, I updated it with a few new flavors and textures like bright cilantro and crunchy pistachios. This particular version is a perfect topping for grilled swordfish, asparagus, roasted potatoes, and shrimp.

In a small bowl, combine the garlic, pistachios, parsley, cilantro, olive oil, salt, lemon zest, lemon juice, and red pepper flakes and stir thoroughly to combine. Use immediately.

Paleo

Whole30

Gluten-Free

Vegan

Vegetarian

Dairy-Free

# Dairy-Free Magic Ranch

Makes 1¼ cups

1 cup 1-Minute Mayonnaise
(page 195)

2½ tablespoons unsweetened
almond milk

1 garlic clove, chopped

½ teaspoon salt

¼ teaspoon freshly ground
black pepper

¼ teaspoon onion powder

¼ teaspoon garlic powder

1 tablespoon chopped fresh dill

1 tablespoon chopped fresh parsley

2 teaspoons chopped fresh chives

I love ranch dressing. I think it makes everything better—pizza, vegetables, chicken, you name it. That means I'm a ranch snob, a purist. It's also why this dairy-free version is also coconut-free; I didn't want a hint of coconut taste in it, just the cool, savory flavor we all know and love. From one ranch snob to another, this is my gift to you.

In a blender or food processor, combine the mayonnaise, almond milk, garlic, salt, pepper, onion powder, and garlic powder. Blend on high for 20 seconds, or until the dressing is smooth. Add the dill, parsley, and chives and pulse five or six times, until the herbs are incorporated. Use immediately or cover and store in the refrigerator for up to 1 week.

Paleo
Whole30
Gluten-Free
Vegetarian
Dairy-Free

# Chipotle Crema

Makes ½ cup

½ cup 1-Minute Mayonnaise
(page 195)

1 garlic clove, minced

2 teaspoons unsweetened
almond milk

1 teaspoon fresh lime juice

½ teaspoon ground chipotle

½ teaspoon salt

I'm not even joking when I say that I add this magical sauce to everything. *Everything.* Eggs, tacos, grilled shrimp, salads. I'm convinced you can add it to any dish for an extra pop of flavor.

In a medium bowl, combine the mayonnaise, garlic, almond milk, lime juice, chipotle, and salt. Use an immersion blender to blend until smooth. Use immediately or cover and store in the refrigerator for up to 1 week.

Paleo
Whole30
Gluten-Free
Dairy-Free
Nut-Free

# Cilantro Guacamole

## Makes 1½ cups

2 ripe large Hass avocados

1 garlic clove, minced

¼ cup chopped fresh cilantro

2 teaspoons fresh lime juice

¼ teaspoon smoked paprika

½ teaspoon salt

Pinch of red pepper flakes

1 tablespoon pine nuts, toasted
(see Tip, page 102)

The first time I made this guacamole, the addition of the pine nuts was completely accidental. I was making fajitas and enlisted the help of our then five-year-old. I asked her to add the pine nuts to our side salad, but they ended up in the guacamole instead. Ohh, the wonders of having "helpers" in the kitchen . . . but it worked! Who knew the nuttiness of the pine nuts could be such a complement to the cool freshness of the avocados?

In medium bowl, combine the avocados, garlic, cilantro, lime juice, smoked paprika, salt, and red pepper flakes. Use a fork to mash the mixture until well combined but still slightly chunky. Stir in the pine nuts. Use immediately.

Paleo

Whole30

Gluten-Free

Vegan

Vegetarian

Dairy-Free

Nut-Free

# Dairy-Free Green Goddess Dressing

## Makes 1½ cups

1 cup 1-Minute Mayonnaise (page 195)

¼ cup unsweetened almond milk

4 anchovy fillets packed in oil, drained

2 garlic cloves

2 tablespoons chopped fresh parsley

2 tablespoons chopped fresh basil

1 tablespoon chopped fresh chives

2 teaspoons chopped fresh tarragon

1 teaspoon fresh lemon juice

½ teaspoon salt

½ teaspoon freshly ground black pepper

Not only does this make a great salad dressing, but I also love it as a dip for veggies, especially snap peas, cucumbers, and jicama.

In a blender, combine the mayonnaise, almond milk, anchovies, garlic, herbs, lemon juice, salt, and pepper. Blend on high until smooth. Use immediately or cover and store in the refrigerator for up to 1 week.

Paleo

Whole30

Gluten-Free

Dairy-Free

Nut-Free

# Sweet Treats

# No'tmeal Cookies

Makes 12

1 large egg

¼ cup honey

1 tablespoon unsalted butter, at room temperature

1½ cups almond flour

½ cup tapioca flour

¼ cup coconut sugar

2 tablespoons unsweetened shredded coconut

1 tablespoon ground golden flaxseed

1½ teaspoons ground cinnamon

1 teaspoon baking powder

⅛ teaspoon salt

½ cup raisins

I've had so many people make these cookies from my blog, and the feedback I continuously get is that they're better than "real" oatmeal cookies. There's no bigger compliment someone can give me. Enjoy these!

Preheat the oven to 350°F. Line a large baking sheet with parchment paper.

In a medium bowl, whisk together the egg, honey, and butter until well combined. Set aside.

In a separate large bowl, thoroughly combine the almond flour, tapioca flour, coconut sugar, shredded coconut, flaxseed, cinnamon, baking powder, and salt. Add the egg mixture and stir to combine well. Add the raisins and stir to incorporate.

Scoop a mound of about 1½ tablespoons of the cookie dough and plop (yes, *plop* . . . it's fun!) it onto the prepared baking sheet. Repeat with the remaining dough, leaving about 2 inches of space between each mound.

Bake for 12 minutes, or until the edges are lightly browned. Let cool for 3 minutes on the baking sheet, then transfer to a wire rack to cool completely before serving. Store in an airtight container for up to 3 days.

Gluten-Free

Vegetarian

# Blueberry Cheesecake Yogurt Pops

### Serves 4 to 6

2 cups dairy-free vanilla yogurt
(I like Kite Hill almond milk yogurt)

1 tablespoon honey

1 teaspoon grated lemon zest

½ cup fresh blueberries

There's no cheese and there's no cake, but when my friend and unofficial taste tester Teresa tried these out, she swore they were the real-deal cheesecake pops. I dare you to make them and think otherwise.

In a blender, combine the yogurt, honey, and lemon zest and blend until well combined. Add the blueberries and pulse until they are broken down and incorporated but the mixture is not totally smooth.

Pour the mixture into ice pop molds and freeze at least overnight or until ready to serve.

Paleo
Gluten-Free
Vegan
Vegetarian
Dairy-Free

# Dairy-Free Jamocha Almond Fudge Ice Cream

## Serves 4 to 6

2½ cups unsweetened almond milk

1½ cups full-fat coconut milk

⅓ cup plus 2 tablespoons coconut sugar

¼ cup instant espresso powder

¾ cup crushed almonds, plus more for serving

1 cup coconut cream (see Note)

10 ounces dark chocolate pieces

Buying an ice cream maker has got to be one of the best decisions I've made in the kitchen. Okay, fine, in my *life*. I mean, to be able to whip up a delicious dairy-free ice cream, free of junky additives and loads of sugar? In 25 minutes? Whenever I feel like it? Yes, please! The amount of money I save on buying fancy dairy-free ice creams makes this purchase well worth it.

In a large bowl, whisk together the almond milk, coconut milk, coconut sugar, and espresso powder until the sugar has dissolved. Pour the mixture into an ice cream maker and churn according to the manufacturer's instructions. Add the crushed almonds 2 minutes before the ice cream is ready.

While the ice cream is churning, in a small saucepan, combine the coconut cream and chocolate pieces. Heat gently over medium heat, stirring frequently, until the chocolate has completely melted, 3 to 4 minutes. Pour the chocolate into a glass jar or bowl and let cool to room temperature.

Transfer half the ice cream to a 2-quart freezer-safe container. Drizzle ¼ cup of the chocolate over the top and use a small spoon to gently swirl it into the ice cream. Transfer the remaining ice cream into the container and swirl in an additional ¼ cup of the chocolate. Reserve the remaining chocolate for serving. Cover and freeze the ice cream for 2 to 4 hours for firmer ice cream or enjoy right away for a soft serve–like consistency.

To serve, scoop the ice cream into individual dishes and top with additional chocolate and crushed almonds.

**Note** *You can easily make your own coconut cream at home by placing a can of full-fall coconut milk in the refrigerator for 5 to 6 hours. The fat solids from the coconut milk will separate from the coconut water, and you can scrape the rich and slightly sweet coconut cream right out of the can.*

Gluten-Free
Vegetarian
Vegan
Dairy-Free

# Apple Stacks

Makes 1

¼ cup salted cashew butter

1 Granny Smith apple, cored and cut crosswise into 4 rounds

2 tablespoons coconut butter, melted

¼ cup dried cranberries

¼ cup walnut pieces

3 teaspoons honey

3 teaspoons unsweetened shredded coconut

When I get a craving for something sweet, this apple stack always does the trick. While it's still definitely a sweet treat, it doesn't leave me feeling the adverse effects that something like a slice of cheesecake would. Needless to say, it makes a great after-school snack for the kiddos.

Spread 1 tablespoon of the cashew butter onto a slice of apple. Drizzle 1½ teaspoons of the coconut butter over the cashew butter and top with 1 tablespoon of the dried cranberries and 1 tablespoon of the walnut pieces. Drizzle the apple slice with ¾ teaspoon of the honey and sprinkle ¾ teaspoon of the shredded coconut over the top. Repeat to make 3 additional slices.

Stack the slices on top of one another and serve.

Paleo
Gluten-Free
Vegan
Vegetarian
Dairy-Free

# Chocolate Chip + Sea Salt Cookies

Serves 8 to 10

1 cup almond flour

2 tablespoons coconut flour

2 tablespoons tapioca flour

½ teaspoon baking soda

1 vanilla bean, split lengthwise and seeds scraped, or ½ teaspoon pure vanilla extract

Pinch of sea salt, plus more for sprinkling

5 tablespoons unsalted butter, at room temperature

½ cup plus 1 tablespoon coconut sugar

1 large egg

1 tablespoon unsweetened almond milk

½ cup semisweet chocolate chunks

Quite frankly, I'm not a huge fan of Paleo or grain-free baking. I feel the results are often tasteless compared to their traditional counterparts and can contain a million hard-to-find ingredients. So when I create a baking recipe, it's a must that the ingredients be easy to find and that the final product won't leave you longing for its gluten- and sugar-laden cousin.

Preheat the oven to 350°F. Line a large baking sheet with parchment paper.

In a large bowl, combine the almond, coconut, and tapioca flours. Add the baking soda, vanilla bean seeds, and salt and stir to combine.

In a separate large bowl using a handheld mixer, whip the butter on medium speed until softened and pale yellow in color. (You could also do this in the bowl of a stand mixer fitted with the paddle attachment.) Add the coconut sugar and whip until combined.

Slowly add the flour mixture to the bowl with the butter and sugar, mixing thoroughly to combine and scraping down the sides of the bowl as needed. Add the egg and almond milk and mix thoroughly.

Place the chocolate chunks in a small zip-top plastic bag and seal. Gently smash the bag with a rolling pin or the bottom of a small pan to break up the chunks, then add the chocolate to the cookie dough. Mix with a spoon until just combined.

Use a fork to scoop a mound of about 1½ tablespoons of the cookie dough and drop it onto the prepared baking sheet. Repeat with the remaining dough, leaving about 2 inches between each cookie.

Bake for 10 minutes, then remove the baking sheet from the oven and gently flatten each cookie with the back of the fork. Sprinkle each cookie with a tiny pinch of sea salt. Bake for 3 to 5 minutes more, until the edges of the cookies have browned slightly. Transfer the cookies to a wire rack and let cool before serving.

Gluten-Free

Vegetarian

# Baked Apples

Serves 4

4 Granny Smith apples

¼ cup coconut sugar

¼ cup gluten-free oats

¼ cup walnut pieces

¼ cup dried cranberries

2 tablespoons salted butter or coconut oil, melted

1 tablespoon unsweetened shredded coconut

1 tablespoon ground golden flaxseed

½ teaspoon ground cinnamon

Pinch of salt

I'm not going to say these apples would be amazing served up with some ice cream, because, frankly, they don't need it—even though I know you're itching to do it! These are amazing as is, but the struggle is real and the choice is yours.

Preheat the oven to 375°F.

Carefully core the apples but do not cut all the way through the bottom. You want a roughly 2-inch-wide cavity. Set aside.

In a small bowl, thoroughly combine the coconut sugar, oats, walnuts, cranberries, butter, coconut, flaxseed, cinnamon, and salt. Stuff one-quarter of the filling into each apple.

Fill an 8-inch square baking pan with ½ inch of water. Place the apples upright in the pan and bake for 45 minutes, until the apples are tender but not falling apart. Transfer to individual bowls and serve.

Gluten-Free

Vegan

Vegetarian

Dairy-Free

# Peaches 'n' Cream

Serves 2 to 4

½ cup full-fat coconut milk, at room temperature

2 medium fresh peaches, peeled, pitted, sliced into wedges, and frozen overnight

1 tablespoon honey, for serving

⅛ teaspoon ground cinnamon, for serving

This is one of my absolute favorite sweet treats, particularly in the summer months when it's too hot to bake or do *anything* in the kitchen, for that matter. It's so easy to make ahead to have on hand for when you're craving a little something sweet. Feel free to try this with a variety of other fruits; frozen cherries, blueberries, and raspberries are great choices, too.

While I prefer to freeze fresh fruit, you can also use pre-frozen fruit if it's out of season in your area.

Line a dinner plate with parchment paper.

Pour the coconut milk into a small bowl. Dip a frozen peach wedge two-thirds of the way into the milk and slowly pull it out, letting the milk freeze over the peach. Transfer to the parchment-lined plate and repeat with the remaining peach wedges. Reserve the remaining coconut milk.

Place the peach wedges in the freezer for 10 minutes to solidify the coconut milk.

Dip each peach wedge in the coconut milk for a second coat and freeze again for 10 minutes more or until ready to serve.

When ready to serve, remove the peach wedges from the freezer, drizzle with the honey, and sprinkle with the cinnamon.

Paleo
Gluten-Free
Vegan
Vegetarian
Dairy-Free
Nut-Free

# Rosé Gummies

Serves 3 or 4

½ cup no-sugar-added white grape juice

2 teaspoons honey

1 teaspoon no-sugar-added dark red fruit juice, such as cranberry, pomegranate, or cherry

2 tablespoons powdered gelatin

½ cup rosé wine

Yes way to rosé gummies! While most people think of gummies as a kid thing, I'm here to bust the lid off that myth. These gummies are exclusively for adults, and they make the perfect treat for such grown-up activities as book club (because who talks about the book, anyway?), bridal showers, and Thursday afternoons when you're ready for the week to be over.

I love the variety of silicone molds available today. Not only do they come in a variety of shapes and sizes, but they make popping your gummies out a breeze. Pick your favorite and enjoy!

In a small saucepan, combine the white grape juice, honey, and red fruit juice. Heat over medium heat, stirring continuously, until the honey has dissolved and the juice is hot but not boiling, about 3 minutes. Very slowly sprinkle in the gelatin, whisking continuously to prevent any lumps from forming. Once all the gelatin is incorporated, pour in the rosé and stir to combine. Cook until just combined and warmed through, 20 to 30 seconds; you do not want to burn off the alcohol. Remove from the heat and pour the mixture into a large glass measuring cup.

Use a spoon to skim any foam or clumps off the top. Pour into silicone candy molds and refrigerate for 2 hours, or until set.

Remove from the molds and serve. Store refrigerated up to 4 days.

Gluten-Free
Dairy-Free
Nut-Free

# Margarita Ice Pops

Serves 6

2 cups diced fresh or frozen mango

¾ cup fresh lime juice
(from about 6 limes)

½ cup honey

⅓ cup your favorite tequila

¼ teaspoon chili powder

1 tablespoon coarse or flaky salt,
for garnish

What's better than a nice cold margarita on a hot day? How about a nice cold margarita on a stick?! Everything's better on a stick, right? Well, maybe not everything, but margaritas definitely are. These ice pops are perfect for parties or just hanging out on your porch. You can also feel free to make these "virgin" pops, aka regular ice pops, by omitting the tequila—they'll still be refreshing and tasty.

In a blender, combine the mango, lime juice, honey, tequila, ½ teaspoon of the chili powder, and ¼ cup water. Blend on high until the mixture is fully combined and smooth.

Pour the mixture into ice pop molds and freeze for at least 8 hours or until ready to serve.

When ready to serve, combine the salt and remaining ½ teaspoon chili powder in a shallow dish. Remove the margarita pops from the molds one at a time and gently press the sides of the pops into the seasoned salt to lightly coat. Enjoy immediately.

Gluten-Free
Nut-Free
Dairy-Free

# Drinks + Beverages

# Apple Cider Vinegar Tonic

2 tablespoons apple cider vinegar

1 teaspoon fresh lemon juice

2 teaspoons honey

1 cup sparkling water, chilled

We all know the benefits of apple cider vinegar, but the taste can be a bit pungent for some. While I wanted to neutralize the pungency with a bit of sweetness, I didn't want this drink to taste like a sugar bomb. So I found just the right ratio of ingredients to balance out the flavors. It's a great alternative to high-sugar juices, and even my vinegar-shy girls love it.

In a glass, stir together the vinegar and lemon juice. Add the honey and stir until it has dissolved. Top off with the sparkling water and stir to combine.

Paleo
Gluten-Free
Vegan
Vegetarian
Dairy-Free
Nut-Free

# Orange Cold-Buster Smoothie

Serves 2

1 cup unsweetened almond milk

½ cup Homemade Chicken Bone Broth (page 182)

1 large orange

1 frozen peeled banana, quartered

1 medium carrot, quartered crosswise

1 (2-inch) piece fresh turmeric, peeled, or 1 teaspoon ground turmeric powder

1 (1-inch) piece fresh ginger, peeled

½ teaspoon pure vanilla extract

Once you get down to the second ingredient in this recipe, you're liable to shut this book and declare that I've lost my damn mind. But I haven't, I swear. I mean, it *is* a cold-busting smoothie, after all. These days, we've all heard about the healing properties of bone broth, but in a smoothie? Yep, I went there. Quite frankly, you aren't going to taste it. And don't wait until you're sick to enjoy this one—I make it on the regular to *keep* me from being laid low.

Combine all the ingredients in a blender and blend on high for 1 minute or until completely smooth.

Paleo
Gluten-Free
Dairy-Free
Nut-Free

# Dairy-Free Latte

## Serves 1

1 cup brewed coffee

¼ cup unsweetened almond milk

1 tablespoon coconut oil

2 teaspoons pure maple syrup

½ teaspoon ground cinnamon

Once you start making this dairy-free latte at home, you'll never feel the need to spend $5 on a coffee shop version again. You don't need a fancy machine to get a creamy, frothy latte—just a blender to whip it all together.

In a blender, combine the coffee, milk, coconut oil, maple syrup, and cinnamon and blend on high until frothy. Pour into a mug and enjoy.

 **Note** *To modify for Whole30, omit the maple syrup.*

Paleo

Whole30-
Compliant If
Modified

Gluten-Free

Vegan

Vegetarian

Dairy-Free

# Matcha Latte

1 cup unsweetened almond milk

½ cup full-fat coconut milk

1 tablespoon honey

1 teaspoon coconut oil

¼ teaspoon pure vanilla extract

1 teaspoon matcha powder

Making a traditional matcha latte can be a bit of a process in terms of time and special equipment, and while I can appreciate the ritual, I don't have the time and patience for it. I mean, trust me—waking up and appreciating the fine art of latte-making without having to ensure (for the twentieth time) that the kids have their homework in their backpacks and that their hair is somewhat brushed and their shoes match is on my bucket list. But until then, blender lattes are where it's at.

In a medium saucepan, combine the almond milk, coconut milk, honey, coconut oil, and vanilla. Heat over medium heat, whisking occasionally, for 6 to 7 minutes, making sure the mixture does not come to a boil.

Pour the mixture into a blender and add the matcha powder. Blend on high for 5 to 10 seconds, until the latte is combined and slightly frothy. Serve immediately.

**Note** *To modify for Whole30, omit the honey and use vanilla bean seeds from one pod instead.*

Paleo

Whole30-Compliant If Modified

Gluten-Free

Vegan

Vegetarian

Dairy-Free

# Dairy-Free Golden Milk

Serves 1

1 cup full-fat coconut milk

1 (1-inch) piece fresh turmeric, peeled and finely grated, or ½ teaspoon ground turmeric

1 (½-inch) piece fresh ginger, peeled and finely grated, or ¼ teaspoon ground ginger

2 teaspoons honey

1 teaspoon coconut oil

¼ teaspoon ground cinnamon

⅛ teaspoon ground cardamom

⅛ teaspoon freshly grated nutmeg

Freshly ground black pepper

Golden milk is all the rage these days. But what exactly *is* it? In short, it's a combination of milk, coconut oil, and the anti-inflammatory spice turmeric. Its roots are founded in the ancient branch of Indian medicine known as Ayurveda, and it's believed to aid in the treatment of a variety of ailments. Medical claims aside, this lightly sweetened, dairy-free version is a warm, comforting, and downright delicious drink that's a great way to squeeze additional nutrients into your diet.

In a small saucepan, combine the coconut milk, turmeric, ginger, honey, coconut oil, cinnamon, cardamom, nutmeg, and ½ cup water. Heat over medium heat until the milk comes to a boil, 4 to 5 minutes.

Transfer the mixture to a blender and blend on high for 15 seconds, or until the ingredients are combined and the milk is slightly frothy.

Pour the golden milk into a mug and top with a pinch of freshly ground black pepper. Enjoy.

**Note** *To modify for Whole30, omit the honey.*

Paleo

Whole30-Compliant If Modified

Vegetarian

Vegan

Dairy-Free

Nut-Free

# Salty Downward Dog

### Serves 2

1 tablespoon coarse sea salt

1½ cups fresh grapefruit juice
(from 3 grapefruits)

1 cup grapefruit-flavored sparkling
water (such as LaCroix, but it's called
"pamplemousse" in LaCroix land)

Social events can be difficult to maneuver on a Whole30 if you aren't prepared. I always suggest bringing something compliant to share in these types of situations. This beautiful mocktail is a great example of that, and it's quite versatile. It's festive and fresh as is if you're looking to avoid alcohol, or can easily be turned into a cocktail for others by adding two shots of gin.

Spread the salt over a small plate. Lightly wet the rims of two glasses (I like to use the leftover rinds from the grapefruit to do this) and gently dip into the salt to coat.

Combine the grapefruit juice and ginger in a shaker and shake to combine and infuse the ginger well.

Fill two glasses halfway with ice, then pour over the grapefruit juice. Top each drink with ½ cup of the sparkling water. Gently stir and serve.

Paleo
Gluten-Free
Vegan
Vegetarian
Dairy-Free
Nut-Free

# Peach + Basil Margarita Mocktail

Serves 4

3 medium fresh peaches, peeled, pitted, and sliced

2 teaspoons honey

2 cups crushed ice

4 medium limes: 3 juiced and 1 sliced into wedges

4 fresh basil leaves

1 tablespoon coarse, flaky salt, for garnish

When it comes to creating a mocktail, I approach it the same way I do a recipe: I try to find complementary flavor combinations between fresh ingredients, then keep the steps simple and the sugar to a minimum. This fruity drink is the perfect example of that—you get the bright, fresh flavors from the peach and herbs without too much sweetness to get in the way. If you'd like to make this into a traditional cocktail, simply add 4 ounces of tequila blanco.

In a blender, combine the peach slices and honey and blend on high for 10 seconds, or until the peaches are completely pureed. Add the ice and lime juice and blend on medium speed for 15 seconds, or until the ice has broken down and the consistency is slushy. Add the basil and pulse four or five times, until the leaves are finely chopped and incorporated.

When ready to serve, spread the salt over a shallow dish. Wet the rim of a glass with a lime wedge and gently dip it into the salt to coat. Repeat with three additional glasses. Divide the drink among the glasses, garnish with a lime wedge, and serve immediately.

Paleo
Gluten-Free
Vegan
Vegetarian
Dairy-Free
Nut-Free

# Minsk Mule

1 tablespoon fresh lime juice
(from about 1 lime)

½ teaspoon honey

1 (½-inch) piece fresh ginger,
peeled and finely grated

Ice

½ cup ginger kombucha

1 ounce sparkling water

Everyone's heard of the Moscow Mule, but what about its health-conscious cousin, the Minsk Mule? No? Well, that's because, like the LA-bred Moscow Mule, it's not from Russia at all, but California—my Bay Area kitchen, to be exact. I make it with ginger kombucha and a touch of honey rather than sugar-loaded ginger beer, and it's delicious. If you'd like to add a bit of alcohol and turn this into a cocktail, add 1½ ounces of gluten-free vodka.

In a measuring cup, stir together the lime juice and honey until the honey has dissolved. Add the ginger. Pour the mixture into an ice-filled glass or copper mule mug. Top with the ginger kombucha and sparkling water and enjoy.

Paleo
Gluten-Free
Vegetarian
Dairy-Free
Nut-Free

# No'jito

½ cup coconut-flavored sparkling water (I love LaCroix)

¼ cup full-fat coconut milk

1 tablespoon fresh lime juice (from about 1½ lime)

4 or 5 fresh mint leaves, plus more for garnish

Ice

Does life get any better than this No'jito mocktail? I think not. This beverage is completely unsweetened and absolutely perfect for hot summer days when you need a refreshing drink that won't leave you feeling like you were hit with a sugar stick. All that, *and* it tastes like sitting on a quiet beach all alone. To *really* get your fake tropical vacay started, add a shot of white rum—just know that your Whole30-compliant NO'jito will then become a decidedly un-Whole30-compliant MO'jito.

In a measuring cup, stir together the sparkling water, coconut milk, and lime juice.

Using a muddler or the handle of a wooden spoon, lightly mash the mint leaves into the bottom of a glass and fill it three-quarters of the way with ice. Pour the No'jito over the ice and enjoy immediately, garnished with additional mint leaves.

Paleo

Whole30

Gluten-Free

Vegan

Vegetarian

Dairy-Free

Nut-Free

# Dairy-Free Strawberry Lassi

Serves 2

2 cups hulled and quartered fresh strawberries

1 cup plain nondairy yogurt

½ cup unsweetened almond milk

2 tablespoons honey

1 teaspoon ground cardamom, plus more for garnish

When the weather gets warm, all my kids want are ice pops and ice cream. Rather than give in to their whims, I make them this cool, fruity alternative that's simple, fresh, and much lower in sugar. Feel free to swap out the strawberries for mangoes or blueberries.

In a blender or food processor, combine the strawberries, yogurt, milk, honey, and cardamom and blend until smooth. Divide between two glasses, garnish with additional cardamom, and serve.

Paleo
Gluten-Free
Vegan
Vegetarian
Dairy-Free

# Index

Note: Page references in *italics* indicate photographs.